Tony and Me

Vince

Tony and Me

A STORY OF FRIENDSHIP

Best Wishes

Jack Klugman

with Burton Rocks

Jack Klugman

GOOD HILL PRESS
WEST LINN, OREGON

Published by Good Hill Press
19363 Willamette Dr. PMB #232
West Linn, Oregon 97068-2010

Library of Congress Cataloging-in-Publication Data

Klugman, Jack. Tony and me : a story of friendship / by Jack Klugman ;
        with Burton Rocks. [West Linn, OR : Good Hill Press, 2006]
p. ; cm.   ISBN 10: 0-9768303-0-2
                    ISBN 13: 978-0-9768303-0-6

1. Randall, Tony. 2. Klugman, Jack. 3. Actors—United States—
Biography. I. Title. II. Rocks, Burton.
PN2287.R36 K58 2005 792.02/8/092—dc22 2005-925210

Photo Sources:
Joan Marcus Photography
119 W. 23rd St
New York., N.Y. 10011-2427

Springer Associates Public Relations
Gary Springer
150 Broadway, #506
New York, N.Y. 10036

Personality Photos
P.O. Box 300050
Midwood Station Booklyn, N.Y. 11230-0050
Personalityphotos.com

PRINTED IN THE UNITED STATES OF AMERICA

10 9 8 7 6 5 4 3 2 1

For Tony

Acknowledgments

About a year ago, my father made a bet with me: if he finished writing the first draft of a book about his friendship with Tony Randall, I would help him publish it. I agreed, pretty confident that it would never happen. After all, he wasn't a writer and I wasn't a publisher. It just seemed like one of those things we'd talk about but never actually realize. I should've known my father better than that. He always does exactly what he promises.

The first indication I got that he was serious came when he started working with a writer, Burton Rocks. It was Burton who broke first ground with Jack by helping him sort through thirty years of a great friendship. Together, they assembled a terrific and all-important first draft of *Tony and Me* in February of 2005.

Since then, it seems like an army of people have helped my father collect on his bet. From Garry Marshall who opened his entire library of photos to me (it was Heather Hall who actually had the key) to Lori Marshall who helped compose Garry's foreword—thank you! And to Heather Randall, who not only supplied her blessing but also the family photos and those rare, early shots of Tony as a young man—thank you for your trust.

Many thanks to Fred Walker, Tony's right-hand man at the National Actors Theatre, for pointing me in all the right directions. I owe much gratitude to Joan Marcus, one of those "right directions" and an amazing photographer who either donated or snapped almost every N.A.T. photo in the book. And to her public relations counterpart for the N.A.T., Gary Springer, thanks for the last minute care package of photos.

Many, many thanks to Al Molinaro, John Byner, and Pat Morita, and Elinor Donahue. And for all the *truly* free advice thanks to Shirley Klein, Les Abell, Susan Hayes, Lisa Montanaro, Oren Teicher, Andy Tobias, Sam Gores, Jennifer Glassman, and Lydia Wills. I'm always amazed by how much I depend on the generosity of people I have yet to meet in person.

BIG thanks to Paramount Studios, Larry McAllister and Michael Arkin for their help with the licensing of *The Odd Couple* gag reel footage. The DVD adds a dimension to Jack and Tony's relationship that photos could never capture.

And to my wife, whose patience is matched only by her attention to detail, thanks for the eagle eye and the unconditional support. I regularly depend on them both.

And finally, my deepest love and gratitude to my brother David who predicted for years that the three of us would work on a project together. You were right. Thanks for breathing life into the book when I doubted it, for always listening so deeply, and for continuing to guide me with your vision and intelligence.

It is my hope that people will enjoy reading *Tony and Me* as much I have enjoyed putting it all together. Yes, I lost to my old man, but it's okay. Because after a lifetime of gambling, it might just be that my father has finally placed a bet where everyone wins.

Adam Klugman

Contents

Foreword

by

Garry Marshall

I t has been more than thirty-five years since my writing
partner Jerry Belson and I developed the television series *The Odd Couple* from Neil Simon's play. Despite the
passage of time, whenever someone mentions *The Odd
Couple* I smile like it was yesterday. I went on to create
twelve other prime-time television series, but *The Odd
Couple* remains one of the shows of which I'm most
proud.

At the time, I was pretty new to television and I went to work everyday of the first season scared to death. My title was "Executive Producer" (which today is known as the "show runner") and I desperately wanted to do a good job. Unfortunately, I didn't even know what a "good job" looked like.

One thing I *did* know was that people were looking to me for answers and I had to be ready with them. I had to make a decision right or wrong. There were a few things, however, I was sure of: I knew a good joke from a bad one and I recognized talent when I saw it. So, when it came to casting *The Odd Couple* I was very clear about my choice of Tony and Jack. The final decision came after a few potentially disastrous casting considerations such as Mickey Rooney in the part of Oscar and Dean Martin as Felix. But, from the moment I envisioned Jack and Tony in the parts, there was never a second thought.

As you might suspect, Jack and Tony were more different than two actors could possibly be: one liked to yell, and the other hated yelling. One dressed in rumpled clothing; the other preferred tailored suits and crisp white button-down shirts. One liked sports; and the other liked opera. One called his bookie; the other called his wife. But the truly amazing part was that their differences never interfered with our work. Jack and Tony were consummate professionals who set a high bar not only for me, but also for the entire cast and crew who proudly followed their lead.

One of my favorite stories about *The Odd Couple* occurred on the very first day of shooting. We were on location in New York filming the opening credits. As we prepared a shot, Tony and Jack waited in a limousine together. After a few minutes Tony suddenly bolted out of the limo and said, "I can't possibly sit in a limousine with this man. He smokes! I can't have smoke going up my nose. It irritates my sinuses! If my sinuses get irritated, I have a sinus attack and I make odd noises and people stare at me. Thusly, I quit."

Then Jack bolted out the other side of the limousine and said, "I can't sit here with this finicky pain in the ass. He keeps complaining about my smoking. I'm a smoker! I like to smoke! That's it. I quit the show." My only thought was: and this is just the first day!

"Wait a second," I said. "Nobody is quitting. Let's talk about it this."

They waited for me to make a decision. I was the boss. I had to make a decision right or wrong. Instinctively, I knew that I shouldn't take sides. So, I said quietly, "You're both right."

They seemed a little startled that I would agree with both of them.

"We are?" they asked.

"Yes. We've made a terrible mistake. And that's why we're going to hire a second limousine. One will be smoking for Jack, and the other will be non-smoking for Tony," I said. "Okay?"

There was silence. Then, much to my relief, they both smiled and agreed to my new plan.

"Okay." I said. "Let's get back to work."

Along with settling the argument, I also learned a valuable lesson: sometimes you can just fix a problem by throwing money at it. In this case, we had the extra money for the second limousine, and I considered it money well spent. If not, I would have paid for it myself because I would've done anything to diffuse the limo war.

Tony would often use my inexperience against me. "Garry," he would say, "no offense . . . but Jack and I have over forty years of combined experience in show business. You have *one*. We win." But that was the exception rather than the rule, because on *The Odd Couple* we were surrounded by brilliant minds, including Jerry Belson, Jerry Paris, Harvey Miller, Bob Brunner, Lowell Ganz, and Mark Rothman.

During the five seasons of *The Odd Couple*, I wrote some of the episodes; I directed some of the episodes; and I produced them all. And one of my greatest pleasures was to watch Tony and Jack take a successful professional relationship and shape it into a deeply personal one.

I was never happier than in this creative Camelot called *The Odd Couple*. I'd like to think that was true for Jack and Tony also. It's very rare to have that kind of relationship on a television series. After reading this book perhaps you'll understand why.

Garry Marshall

Tony and Me

*Backstage at the National Actors Theatre
Benefit Performance of* The Odd Couple, 1991.

CHAPTER 1

The Start of a Beautiful Friendship

The day Tony died a reporter asked me to comment. I said that a world without Tony Randall is a world I will never be able to recognize; it is certainly one I will never accept.

A few days later, it occurred to me that maybe what I said was an overstatement. Now many, many months have gone by and I realize that what I said is truer than ever: I *cannot* recognize the world without Tony Randall in it, and I will never accept it. The other day my phone rang and I found myself insisting that when I picked it up I would hear his warm, resonant tone: "Hello, Jack! Tony calling!"

* * *

I first saw Tony Randall on the Mr. *Peepers* live television show in the early fifties and became an instant fan. When I finally had the chance to work with him a few years later it was milestone for me. It was 1954 on a summer replacement show for *Goodyear Theatre* called *Appointment with Adventure*. At that time, *Goodyear Theatre* did original scripts and adaptations of great books by great authors like Hemingway, Faulkner, Huxley, etc. It was considered a classy show, and it was. At least it was for nine months of the year.

The remaining three months were full of potboilers and stinkers and it so happened that Tony and I starred in one of those stinkers. He played a professor and I played a gangster (So what else was new?). The characters had one thing in common— they both loved to cook. The show was broadcast live and that was always exciting; unfortunately, our performances and the writing were not.

Many years later, it became a kind of joke between us. In the seventies, when we were interviewed as the "Odd Couple," Tony used to get a kick out of kidding the interviewer about our past performances. He would explain how spectacular we were in this wonderful show called *Appointment with Adventure*, after which he would hold his nose and laugh loudly until the interviewer got it that Tony was kidding around. God, how I loved to hear Tony laugh! It was a loud, bawdy laugh, conveying everything a laugh should—that the laugher is having a ball.

In the 1950s Tony played a professor to my gangster in
Appointment with Adventure. *So what else was new?*
Gangsters were my bread and butter for years.

THE START OF A BEAUTIFUL FRIENDSHIP | 3

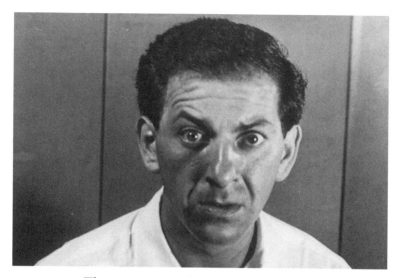

This was my very first promotional photo.
No wonder I wasn't getting the leading man roles!

During the next seventeen years I only saw Tony in movies and television. I didn't actually meet him again until the first rehearsal for the first episode of *The Odd Couple* in 1970. We all got together in Garry Marshall's office for the first read-through of the first script. There was a moment where I made the choice to have Oscar Madison yell at Felix Unger. When the reading was over everyone went to lunch except Garry, Tony, and me. Garry said he thought the reading went well. Tony agreed, except that he thought Oscar shouldn't shout at Felix at that time.

"Why not?" I asked.

"Because it's wrong," Tony insisted. "Well, you're not going to shout when we do it, are you?" he asked.

"I don't know. I might," I told him. "That's what this

rehearsal is for. I might holler even louder, or I may not. I'll see."

"No! No! You *mustn't* shout. You just can't!" Tony said forcefully.

I turned to Garry and said, "Look, we've just gotten started here and it hasn't cost anybody anything, except for my plane fare, which I'll pay back. I just can't work this way."

"What way?" Tony asked.

"With you telling me how to act," I said to Tony.

"Why not?" he quipped.

"Because I would never tell *you* how to act," I returned. "I wouldn't have that kind of chutzpah. I don't let anybody mess around with my acting," I told him. Tony sensed he shouldn't pursue it any further because he shrugged his shoulders and said:

"Fine, okay. I was just trying to help."

I thought that was the end of it.

Four weeks later, however, we were working on the fourth episode of *The Odd Couple* and everything was going very well. Then, out of nowhere, Tony turned to me and said, "Why can't I tell you what to do when I think you've made the wrong choice?"

"*Now*" I said, laughing a bit, "you can tell me anything you want."

"Why? What's different now?" he asked me. "What's changed?"

"Now it's a *suggestion*, not an order," I said. Tony understood immediately: he could offer any suggestion he wanted to so long as he understood that *I didn't have to take it.* I'm not sure how the show would've turned out if Tony and I had gotten into a power struggle around that issue. Thank God we didn't, because the mutual respect we established that day was, in many ways, the seed of our long and successful collaboration.

Not to mention, Tony gave me some of my funniest bits!

The Odd Couple, *1974 "The Big Broadcast."*
Over the years, Tony gave me some of my funniest bits.

The Sunshine Boys, *National Actors Theatre*, *1998*.

Maybe the most famous scene from the play, The Odd Couple.
Felix says, "It's not a spoon you ignoramus, it's a ladle!"

CHAPTER 2

A Tale of
Two Actors

Jack

I'm a gambler. I've always been a gambler, and I will always be a gambler. By the time I was ten years old I knew enough about every kind of gambling to lose several fortunes, and over the years, I probably have. Today, I bet only on horses, and not very successfully. As Joe E. Lewis once said, "I follow horses that follow horses." It's pure fun for me now because my bets are very small and so are my losses. These days I'm in charge of my gambling—it isn't in charge of me.

This was not always the case.

In 1945 I had saved three thousand dollars in U.S. Savings Bonds—all of which I lost betting on baseball games. I was twenty-three years old and by today's standards I would say it was equal to losing about twenty-five or thirty grand—*a lot* of money! And to make matters worse, I owed the local loan shark five hundred dollars!

At first, I thought the loan shark debt wasn't going to be a big problem because his nephew Henry was my best friend. I even used to call the loan shark, "Uncle Tommy." But when I was unable to pay him for about a month, Henry informed me that Uncle Tommy had turned my debt over to two "collectors" (Collectors, ha! These guys were thugs!). I had three days to come up with some money or else these collectors were going to come looking for me—and break my legs just for starters.

"Uncle Tommy," I pleaded. "I've always paid you before. Just gimme some time. I just need a little time," I explained.

Tommy looked at me sympathetically and said, "Jake," (This was my nickname growing up in South Philadelphia.) "I've always liked you, but I got a hundred grand on the street right now. You don't pay me what you owe me, word gets out that I didn't do nothin' about it guess what happens? I kiss that hundred grand goodbye. Now you get me some money before they get to you, and I'll try to stop 'em."

Hardly reassuring. I had no way of coming up with

that kind of cash. I knew I had to get out of town—but to where?

I had one bet left to make, but it was definitely a long shot.

* * *

When I was a kid, I would go to the movies alone. On the way home, I would act out some of the scenes I'd just seen.

I remember one time I came home after seeing Wallace Beery and Jackie Cooper in *The Champ*. At the end of the movie, Jackie Cooper, who was only twelve at the time, sobs uncontrollably after "the champ" (played brilliantly by Wallace

Little me, about six or seven, secretly planning to be the next Jackie Cooper.

Beery) dies. Over and over, Jackie Cooper cries, "I want the champ! I want the champ!" All the while, he's pushing through heaving sobs as he screams. It's a remarkable moment.

Anyway, for some unknown, completely unexpected reason I thought I could do what Jackie Cooper had done in *The Champ*. So, I performed the final scene for my family when I got home, and I was good! I even cried real tears! No one was more surprised than I was. Still, my family was unimpressed.

"Look who wants to be an actor?" they laughed. "What are you, Clark Gable?"

Once shamed, I never, *ever* mentioned wanting to be an actor again to anyone.

You have to understand that I grew up in a pretty tough neighborhood in South Philadelphia, and telling people you wanted to be an actor when you grew up was like saying you wanted to be a florist. If you knew what was good for you, you kept your mouth *shut*. In fact, I don't think I ever took *myself* seriously as an actor until Uncle Tommy's "collectors" came looking for me.

Necessity is the mother of invention, I guess, because I suddenly remembered a guy I had met in the service. I don't even remember his name but before World War II he had attended Carnegie Tech (now Carnegie Mellon) as a drama student and loved it. The university was in Pittsburgh, so I would still be in the same state. I could only hope was that it was far enough away so Uncle Tommy's goons wouldn't come looking.

While I was considering all of this, I moped around the house a lot. Finally, my mother couldn't stand it anymore and confronted me—in Yiddish.

"What's wrong, Jake? All day you hang around the house like a dead person."

I wanted to strike out at somebody and since she asked, I let her have it—in English.

"All right, Mom! You want to know what's wrong? I'll tell you exactly what's wrong! Remember the three thou-

*My mother Rose, 1969. She played guilt the
way Jascha Heifetz played the violin.*

sand dollars I had saved up in bonds? Well it's gone! All
of it. I lost it—gambling!"

I watched the blood drain from her face.

"So, what are you going to do?" she said.

"I'm going to college," I blurted. "Carnegie Tech—in
Pittsburgh," I think it was the first time I had ever said it
out loud.

I watched the blood slowly come back to her face.

"*You're* going to go to college?" she said in disbelief.

"Yes," I replied. "*I'm* going to college."

My mother looked me dead in the eye and said bluntly, "It's the best money you ever lost."

Now she watched the blood drain from *my* face. I couldn't believe what she had said! My mother played guilt the way Jascha Heifetz played the violin and here was an opportunity for her to perform an entire concerto in honor of my monumental screw-up, and instead she gave me a pass. It was incredible. I had finally found the one thing she valued more than guilt—and it was *education*.

That night I drove to Pittsburgh and slept in the car.

* * *

The next morning I went to a gas station, washed up, changed shirts, and drove to the main building at Carnegie Tech. I walked up to a pretty girl behind the administrator's desk and explained that I wanted to apply to the acting school. She said my timing was perfect—I was just in time for the audition.

"Audition? For what?" I asked. "Besides, what's an audition?" That's how unsophisticated I was. I had never spoken in front of three people before, much less "auditioned."

"All students who want to take the acting course have to audition to see whether the school will accept them." I told her I wasn't prepared for an audition. She rummaged through her desk and came up with a copy of *Our Town*.

"Here," she said, "study the part of the stage manager and be ready to perform it for the teachers tomorrow." That night I got a local room and studied and studied and studied . . . but to no avail. I didn't know what I was studying *for*!

The next day I walked into the auditorium, only to see twenty-seven eighteen-year-old girls. I was the only guy. Now I should have felt pretty good about those odds, but I didn't. I was extremely anxious and uncomfortable, especially when these girls got up on stage and performed their monologues. It was the first time I'd ever heard the English language spoken that way. And by that, I mean, *properly*. These girls were so accomplished!

I, on the other hand, had grown up on the streets. I was twenty-three years old. I had been in the army. I had run numbers. I had taken bets for a bookie. I was the only Jew in an all-Italian neighborhood and spoke as if I had just left the company of Tony Soprano. In other words, I had been around the block a couple of times and these were not the type of girls I had dated.

(As an aside, some of these girls turned out to be fine actresses, such as Sada Thompson, with whom I later did *All My Sons*, and Nancy Marchand, who played the mother in *The Sopranos*. Both were sensational.)

Suddenly it was my turn to audition. I walked toward the stage slowly on wobbly legs as I tried to become that New England stage manager; but I couldn't make it. I started to hyperventilate, had a full-blown panic attack, and in the middle of my monologue declared that I couldn't go on. I slunk back to my seat, humiliated.

When the auditions were over, we were instructed to go see the teachers in their respective offices in order to receive our evaluations. Mrs. Morris, the head of the department then and a former Broadway star, said to me, bluntly:

"Mr. Klugman, you do not belong here. It is my opinion that you are not suited to be an actor. In fact, I believe you are more suited to be a truck driver, but you see our problem," she continued, "we have no men to do scenes with. Now in January, our boys will be coming back from the Service, and if I accept you today, I may very well let you go later. I'm being this honest with you because I want you to know all the facts."

What choice did I have? If I went back to Philadelphia, I'd get my knees broken! The semester was four months long and I figured I could get a job as a busboy or a waiter and then I'd be able to send some money home to Uncle Tommy. In four months, I could reduce my debt by a lot.

"Mrs. Morris," I said. "I know I don't have the qualifications to be an actor. I just want to give it a shot and get it out of my system."

So, under a kind of probation, I was accepted to Carnegie Tech. I immediately got a job as a busboy in a steak restaurant and sold my jalopy for eighty dollars. But I still had to come up with two hundred and fifty bucks for tuition at Carnegie Tech. I didn't have that kind of money, but thank God I was able to use the G.I. Bill to help pay for that first semester.

After three weeks, I sent Uncle Tommy, through his nephew, a hundred bucks. He had to be happy with that. But he still didn't know where I was because I had asked Henry not to tell him. Thank God Henry obliged me!

So, I found a little apartment in an elderly woman's house and I was, in fact, quite happy. When school started, I was assigned a scene from an old play called *One Sunday Afternoon*. I played a guy who had just been released from prison and was going to meet his girl in the park. I rehearsed the part for three long weeks. I never spent a moment without thinking about that scene. I said the lines while I was working, just before I went to sleep, and when I woke up in the morning. I ate, drank, walked, and lived those lines every minute of every day for three weeks.

Finally, the time came for me to perform the scene. All of the accepted students were in the audience, many of whom had seen me humiliate myself on the very same stage with *Our Town* a few weeks before. There were three chairs on stage, representing the park bench, and two flats that were supposed to be trees.

My acting partner walked on stage while I was in the wings, waiting to make my entrance.

And it is here I must digress for a minute.

I had a rich uncle in Philadelphia, and whenever we went to his house for dinner and he was serving chicken

I'd always say I wasn't hungry—not because I didn't like chicken, but because I didn't know how to *eat* the chicken. No one had ever taught me. I was too embarrassed to pick it up, I didn't know how to cut it and so it was just easier to say I wasn't hungry.

Now, back to the wings at Carnegie Tech. As I was about to make my first real entrance onto a stage, my heart was beating so hard I thought it would break through my skin. My head was spinning, my knees were weak, and I was certain I was going to make a complete ass of myself again. Instead, when I stepped out onto that stage, something remarkable happened—a calm came over me that I had never experienced before. Suddenly the sets and props around me were more real than anything I had known in my so-called "real life."

Those three chairs became a park bench. The two flats became trees. I *truly* loved that girl, and I knew, I *knew* that I could eat chicken on that stage! I had found the place where I belonged. In fact, I discovered that I was more comfortable on stage than I was in life. That is still true today.

I don't even remember getting through the scene because I was on cloud nine during the whole thing. I just remember that when it was over, those twenty-six eighteen-year-old girls were all applauding. A moment later Mrs. Morris stood up and said to the class:

"You see, class," she announced, "I almost made a terrible mistake. I have always expected talent to come in a nice box, wrapped with pretty paper and a beautiful blue ribbon. Well, today I learned that sometimes talent comes in a plain, cardboard box; a box with a lot of dirt on it." Then Mrs. Morris turned to me and said, "Mr. Klugman, I was wrong. You certainly *do* belong here."

I felt my eyes start to fill up with tears. I ran off the stage and back to my apartment where I enjoyed the happiest cry of my life. That was the day acting became my best friend.

Tony

I've always promised myself that if I ever wrote a book, I would never do two things: kiss and tell, and bore people with long histories of things. I'm about to break that promise.

So, here's the dirt: Tony Randall has not always been Tony Randall. In fact, he used to be Leonard Rosenberg of Tulsa, Oklahoma—one of about six-and-a-half Jews found in the Midwest during the early 1920s (I'm exaggerating, of course, but only a little bit). He was so private about the fact that he had changed his name that I knew him for twenty years before I found out!

Tony's first experience with theatre is very revealing about him. When he told me the story of the first play he ever saw, he said that he didn't even remember the name of it. He was thirteen years old and he only remembers

*Leonard Rosenberg with
his mother in Tulsa,
Oklahoma, 1940.*

coming away with one, quiet thought: "I can do it better than those actors." It's always been interesting to me how different he and I were that way. As an actor, I started with the question, "Can I do it?" Tony started with the certainty that he could.

From that moment forward, Tony was hooked. After high school, he went directly to Northwestern University where he absorbed theatre like a sponge. He studied speech, dance, fencing, vocal production, drama, literature, music, you name it and Tony threw himself into it.

He molded himself into an actor by training in a classical tradition, where every aspect of the artist's body is in play. After that, there was no question—go east to New York.

And that's what he did, where he quickly fell in with the Neighborhood Playhouse School of Theatre and worked with Sandy Meisner. Now I don't know much about the Meisner Technique, but there was something about it that suited Tony's precise nature perfectly. In fact, Sandy Meisner became his mentor and for the rest of his life Tony remained deeply grateful to the Neighborhood Playhouse for what it had given him. (I heard Tony left a large gift to the Neighborhood Playhouse. It doesn't surprise me. Tony always put his money where his mouth was.)

* * *

During the late 1930s there was a lot of opportunity in radio and Tony quickly built a solid reputation as voice talent. After a couple years in radio, Tony made his Broadway debut in a play called *A Circle of Chalk* and his performance earned him the respect of the New York theatre community. Unfortunately, just as his stage career was lifting off, Tony was drafted into the Signal Corps and it put everything on hold for four years.

When he came home, Tony immediately went back into radio but soon saw New York transformed by a new industry: *live television*. It was here that Tony, like so many of us, became a pioneer.

Creatively, New York was a fantasyland for actors back then. On every street corner was another great play by another gifted American playwright. I remember one time walking from Fifty-Seventh Street to Forty-second taking note of the playwrights being produced on that day: Arthur Miller, Eugene O'Neill, Tennessee Williams, Maxwell Anderson, and Clifford Odets. All within fifteen blocks!

I saw Arthur Miller's *Death of a Salesman* with Lee J. Cobb five times and it is still (in my opinion) the best American play ever written. I saw Tennessee Williams' *A Streetcar Named Desire*, with Marlon Brando *seventeen* times for $1.80 a throw. Can you imagine it? Seeing a young Marlon Brando in *Streetcar*—for $1.80!

Anyway, it was a natural for New York's fledgling television industry to import theatre talent from its own backyard. That's how many of us scraped a living together—by getting small parts in these new television shows. Tony, however, had established himself in New York before the war. He already had an excellent reputation and it helped him land his first big acting job.

It was in a show called *Mr. Peepers*, and he co-starred with another great talent, Wally Cox. They were absolutely brilliant together. Tony played this prissy teacher and he was meticulous. If he had done a little more, it would have been too much; a little less, and there would have been no definable character. It was a high-wire performance and he never lost his balance.

As I said, Mr. *Peepers* was the first time I ever saw Tony in anything and I was instantly impressed. He not only had talent and presence, but I saw that he was an actor who knew his craft. I tell young actors all the time: *learn your craft and the rest will take care of itself.* Tony is a great example of what I mean. He was prepared for the opportunity that Mr. *Peepers* presented and when it came

Tony with the cast of Mr. Peepers, *1954.*
The character he played was a high-wire act
and Tony never lost his balance.

along, it established him as an actor whose star was on the rise.

Tony went on to work with some of the biggest stars of the day; from Katherine Cornell to Paul Muni to Rock Hudson and they all benefited greatly by working with him. He was such a generous actor that everyone he worked with became better, more grounded, more specific. And that's because Tony completely enveloped you with his concentration in a way that I'd never experienced with any other actor before.

I first noticed it while we working on an episode of *The Odd Couple*. I can't remember exactly which show it was, but it called for Tony to be sick. From the minute he walked into rehearsal on Monday to the minute we finished shooting on Friday, Tony *was* sick. He wasn't *playing* sick; he wasn't *acting* sick only when the camera's were rolling. Tony *was* sick and he never dropped it. When we would "wrap" for lunch, Tony wouldn't break character and tell jokes in the commissary. He would slink back to his dressing room like someone who had barely survived the morning.

You see, Tony was a playful soul and that's why acting suited him so perfectly. He was like a kid, always daring me to take the next risk, provoking me into matching his commitment, challenging me to outsmart him. He made me a better actor because he kept me on my toes. Every actor who has ever worked with him will tell you the same.

I mention this because I want to set the record

straight on just how good Tony was. Don't get me wrong, people know Tony was good. But they don't know *how good*. I encourage you to go back to Tony's early work and see what I am talking about. Go back and look at *The Odd Couple*. Watch Tony—he never says a word he doesn't believe; never draws a breath that isn't true. Even now, I learn something new every time I watch him.

It reminds me of when I was working with Ethel Merman on the stage production of *Gyspy*. I especially loved it when she sang to me. One time she caught me smiling at her during a performance. When we were off-stage, she said to me, teasingly:

"I saw you smiling out there. Did you pay to get in?"

"No, baby," I said. "But I've got the best seat in the house."

That's how I feel about the three decades I worked with Tony—like I always had the best seat in the house.

People ask me all the time: "Were you and Tony as different in real life as you were on TV?" and, "Do you think that's why *The Odd Couple* was so successful?" I usually say yes, Tony and I were a lot like our characters but I also add that it was not our differences that made us successful, but our similarities.

The Odd Couple rang true not because I was kind of sloppy in real life and Tony was a little fussy, but because we were both trained actors who had extensive theatre backgrounds. It was our mutual love for acting that allowed us to understand each other, *in spite* of our differ-

With Ethel Merman, circa 1978. When we did Gypsy *on Broadway, I had the best seat in the house every night.*

ences. And when Tony launched his dream of a National Actors Theatre, it was our commitment to the arts and our deep belief in the importance of theatre that brought us together again to raise money. I mention this because I took great comfort in this aspect of our relationship. We had an important professional ally in each other so that even though Tony and I were different in a thousand ways, the core of our success was rooted in our shared values.

In thirty-five years of working together, those values never let us down.

*Live television! That's me on the far left of Bogart,
with the potato sack.* The Petrified Forest, *1954.*

Me with Bogart again, same show, only add my idol
Henry Fonda on the far left.
What a lucky guy I was to work with giants like that!

*I finally got my headshots right, and by the early 1950s
I started getting some great live television gigs.*

Walter Matthau and Art Carney,
The Odd Couple, *Broadway, 1965.*

CHAPTER 3

The Birth of
The Odd Couple

I n 1964, I was doing a series called 90 *Bristol Court*.
Danny Simon, Neil Simon's older brother, was my
script editor. He was very good at his job, but nothing
could save that series and it was cancelled after thirteen
shows.

Danny Simon *was* Felix Unger, a neat hypochondriac
whose wife couldn't stand it anymore and threw him out.
Danny moved in with Roy Gerber, an agent. Roy Gerber
was Oscar Madison. And believe me they lived the life of
The Odd Couple.

After a while, Danny began see the humor in their
differences and decided to write a play about their living

together. Danny and Neil Simon were very close and, in fact, it was Danny who encouraged Neil Simon to become a comedy writer. Danny told Neil his idea for the play and Neil loved it.

"It's a wonderful idea, keep working on it," Neil told him. Six months later, they talked again.

"How's that play coming along?" Neil asked.

"I can't seem to get it to work," Danny told him.

Neil said, "It's such a great idea. How about you let me have a crack at it, and I'll give you ten percent." Wisely, Danny accepted the offer and it made him millions.

Walter Matthau was the first Oscar. He played the part on Broadway opposite Art Carney and he was brilliant. But, not long after they opened, Danny told me that Walter Matthau was leaving for four months to work on the movie, *The Fortune Cookie*, with Jack Lemmon. He asked me if I wanted to take over for Walter. I read the play and laughed so hard I literally fell off the couch. I thought it was sensational and gave Danny an enthusiastic "Yes!"

My agent at the time was Milton Goldman and he negotiated a contract. I got fifteen hundred dollars a week, which was fine with me—even though it bugged me a little that they were paying Walter Matthau *fifty-eight hundred a week*.

When I saw him play Oscar, however, I knew he deserved every penny of that fifty-eight hundred bucks and

I came away knowing I could never match Walter's performance. But I also knew I had to find my own way into this part. But how? Walter was hitting every mark, getting every laugh, touching every nuance. And so I watched him again. And again. And again, until finally I saw it: near the end of the second act, Felix and Oscar are really having it out and Oscar says, ". . . and then you move in, my oldest and dearest friend . . ." That's when it hit me: *this* is the soul of the play.

That was my way in and became the bedrock of every *Odd Couple* performance I ever gave. Now, I'm not saying I was better than Walter, but I did manage to make the part my own, and when you're following a star like Matthau, that's one hell of an accomplishment.

During the filming of *The Fortune Cookie*, Walter had a severe heart attack and was not able to return to *The Odd Couple*. The producer asked me to sign a year's contract and offered me a two hundred and fifty dollar a week raise.

"Make it five hundred dollars a week and I'll do it" (I had never made one hundred thousand dollars in a single year, and I was enticed by the thought of it). Surprisingly, they said no.

"Wait a minute," I said. "Weren't you paying Walter Matthau fifty-eight hundred dollars a week?"

They said, "yes."

"So, you'd still be saving thirty-eight hundred dollars a week. We're packing the house every night!"

The Odd Couple *was one of the first American comedies to be a hit in London. Victor and I played to standing room only for an entire year.*

They still said, "no."

Of course, they never thought I would quit. Even my own agent, Milton Goldman, didn't think I would quit. But I did. I quit the next week.

Four years later, I did *The Odd Couple* in London where it also received rave reviews, which was unusual because American comedies are generally not well received in London. But I wasn't surprised English audiences liked this play. They're sophisticated. And let's face it, it doesn't take a seasoned critic to see that *The Odd Couple* is a brilliant American comedy.

"This ticket will be hotter than Olivier's *Othello*," one of the reviewers said.

He was right. We played to standing room only for an entire year. When Neil Simon finally saw the London show, he wrote a very nice letter to me. Then I heard he went back to America and said to Arnold Saint-Subber, his producer, "Maybe we should have given Jack the extra two hundred and fifty bucks!"

The Odd Couple, *1970, "Scrooge gets an Oscar."*

CHAPTER 4

Collaborating with Tony

W hen it came time to shoot the pilot for *The Odd Couple* series, Tony actually wanted Mickey Rooney to play the part of Oscar. He had done the play with Mickey in summer stock and they had also gotten great notices.

Garry Marshall, who was the Co-Executive Producer of *The Odd Couple*, wanted me to play the part and fought for me. I figured it was because he had seen me on Broadway when I replaced Walter Matthau.

So, a few days into the first rehearsals, I thanked Garry and made a joke about how he must have caught me on a very good night. That's when he said, in his low, slow Bronx accent, something that shocked me:

"I never saw you play Oscar on Broadway."

"What!" I blurted. "Then why did you fight for me?"

"I saw you in *Gypsy*. You did a scene with Ethel Merman and I was impressed because as she was singing to you, she was spitting a lot and it was getting on your clothes and your face and in your eyes. You never even flinched. I said to myself, 'Now that's a good actor.' "

And that's how I got the biggest break of my career. Go figure.

Meanwhile, the wardrobe department was having trouble finding the right clothes for Oscar. No matter what they chose, they couldn't make the producers happy. In fact, it went on for so long that the wardrobe people were starting to panic.

Then one day I walked onto the set for rehearsal and the wardrobe guys came up to me. I noticed they were eyeballing my sport coat and kind of rubbing the fabric between their fingers.

"Listen, Jack" they confided, "We can't find the type of clothes that Oscar would wear and we're running out of time. So, we were thinking . . . what if we bought *your* clothes?"

"What?" I thought they were joking.

"Well, Jack . . . your sport coats . . . are exactly the kind of things we think Oscar would wear." They weren't joking. I didn't know whether to be flattered or insulted.

"Wait a minute. You guys are serious. You really want to *buy* my clothes!" I said.

"Not all of them" one guy kidded, "just your pants, jackets, shirts, and shoes. You can keep your underwear and socks."

"How much?" I asked.

"Three hundred and fifty bucks," one of them said.

"Deal," I said right away. "And I want it in cash."

They smiled and walked away like a couple of bandits. What neither of them knew was that even at three hundred and fifty bucks for *all* of my clothes, I still made a profit!

* * *

We shot the first fifteen shows with one camera and the only good episode centered on an injured parrot that we thought was dead, but was really just in a coma. In my opinion, the rest of them stunk. Apparently, the network agreed with me because after fifteen shows we were cancelled, with not much chance of even finishing the regular season.

Feeling like we hadn't been given a proper shot, we all lobbied the ABC executives, explaining that the show would never work with one camera. We told them that Tony and I were stage actors who loved the rehearsal process and knew how to use it. We said that if we switched from a one camera set up to a three camera set up they would be taking advantage of our strengths.

You see, in a one camera world, you don't get any

rehearsal. Most of the time is spent setting up or breaking down shots and so it takes all week just to get the show in the can. But a three camera world is another thing entirely. If the network would let us do things this way, it would give us all week to rehearse. Then on Friday, we could shoot the show straight through, in front a live audience, with real people and real laughter.

We begged them to let us use the three camera format, literally getting down on our knees to get rid of the damned laugh track. Oh, how we hated that canned laughter! It was an insult. Tony and I knew how to get real laughs! Tony even quoted Fred Allen to one of the execs about laugh tracks, "Do you realize how many of those people laughing are dead?"

The network pushed back and challenged us to prove that there was real interest in the show. So, Tony and I borrowed an office at ABC studios in New York for one week and called almost every newspaper in America. We asked them to tell their readers to write to the network and say how much they hated the laugh track.

Almost overnight, we created a furor, and by the end of the week, we had received more than three hundred thousand letters. The network got the point and let us finish the season with three cameras, a live audience, and *no laugh track!*

Now we had what we needed to give the show a fair shake and we all started having fun; not just Tony and me, but the writers and producers as well as the other ac-

We were surrounded by big talent. For example,
that's a very young Garry Marshall in the middle.

tors were all energized by the live audience. By the end of
the first season, *The Odd Couple* was a show with real legs.

It's no surprise really; we were surrounded by big talent. We had Garry Marshall, Jerry Belson, and Harvey
Miller producing, three of the funniest (and craziest)
people I've ever known. We had Tony and me playing
Felix and Oscar and there was a deep pool of talented reg-
ulars like Penny Marshall, Al Molinaro, Gary Walberg,

In spite of the great work we were doing, The Odd Couple *tanked in the ratings. Tony, lower left. Garry, upper right.*

John Byner, Dick Stahl, and a hundred other talented people who kept me laughing through all those years. Sometimes it's hard to believe I got paid to do it!

However, we still struggled in the ratings. One of the little known facts about *The Odd Couple* is that every year we were on the air, for all five seasons, we were cancelled in June and picked up again two months later in August.

The reason for this is a little complicated. You see, the networks kept airing our show at different times on different nights, so people could never make us a part of their routine; that is during the regular season. During the summer season though, it aired at the same time

From left to right: Me, Co-Executive Producer Jerry Belson, Tony, and Garry, 1972. Jerry had a cynical, off-center sense of humor that helped give the show an authentic New York flair.

*Same day. The guy between Garry's knees is Harvey Miller.
Harvey was a masterful punch-up artist
who supplied the one-liners that always broke me up.*

every week. When people would be flipping past reruns of
shows they'd already seen, they would stop to watch *The
Odd Couple*. They would realize what a good show it
was and would watch it faithfully all summer long. The
ratings would go up and stay up for three months. That's
when the network would change its mind and give us
another season.

It always bugged Tony that we got cancelled every year, even though he understood it wasn't our fault. I told him several times that when the show went into syndication, that's when people would find us, and that's when we'd be a big hit. You can't have that many talented people doing such good work and not be successful. Time will always tell.

Besides, we had nowhere to go but up. And in some ways, Tony and I benefitted from the low ratings. After the second year our agent Abbey Greshler was able to renegotiate our contract and get Tony and me a legitimate piece of the show. ABC never thought it'd be worth anything and so they were overly generous. It turned out to be a very good thing for us. That "piece" sent both of my kids to college.

* * *

During the first rehearsals of *The Odd Couple*, when five o'clock came around, all the writers would meet at a big table to brainstorm. One day, Tony and I showed up. There were quite a few surprised faces.

"You boys are done. Go home," they told us, as if they were letting us off the hook.

"No," we said, "we *want* to be in on the writing."

They laughed.

"No, no, fellas," they said. "You do the acting and we do the writing."

They tried to dismiss us, but Tony was stern.

"No!" he insisted. "This is a collaborative effort. Jack

The writer's table, circa 1972. By this time, the show had hit a good stride and we were all having a great time.

and I have forty years of experience between us. We have a contribution to make and we intend to make it."

I just smiled and backed him up. At this point, they had no real choice. Tony could be a formidable adversary and they could tell he was ready to fight them on it. So, what could they do? They let us have a seat at the table. Eventually, the writers came to respect our input and, in the end, thought of us as an important part of the writing process.

It was only a half-hour show but we all worked every night, Tuesday to Friday, until eleven o'clock. By Friday, maybe six pages of the original script remained. That's why some writers didn't want to write for us. Those that did realized that our changes made the show better.

Tony and I never saw the show as merely a frolic, but rather as a portrait of friendship. We wanted the humor to come from the character interactions. Sometimes, even when really funny lines were handed to us, we would protest.

"These are jokes, fellas! We don't do jokes!" Actors can't play jokes. Actors play intentions. We have to make the relationships real first, or nothing will be believable *or* funny.

Again, these were lessons we'd learned in the theatre and we were constantly going back to them. In fact, each year we had a four-month hiatus and Tony and I would spend ten weeks of that time doing the play, *The Odd Couple*. It was a great way to stay in shape for the television season and I am convinced it improved the work we did on the show.

It seems strange now, but Tony and I didn't socialize much in those days. Even though were on the road together, when a performance was over, we often went our separate ways. Mostly, it was my doing. People don't always believe me when I tell them, but I really am a loner.

An original program from one of The Odd Couple *tours. Very '70s. Tony and I always went back to the theatre.*

It wasn't that I didn't love and admire Tony during those times; I just didn't know how to express it. So, I kept to myself a lot. In time, that would change.

On the road, Tony always demanded that every member of the cast give two hundred percent and whenever he felt we were getting a little bored, he would pull some kind of prank. I remember on more than one occasion Tony would wait for the stage manager to give the five minute signal, then suddenly streak across the stage naked with a roll of toilet paper unfurling behind him. I loved to watch the other cast members as a bare-assed Tony pranced by them with a roll of toilet paper sticking out of his butt. They were stunned, as if they couldn't trust their own eyes. It was so inconsistent with Tony's "proper" persona that they practically had to pinch themselves to see if it was real.

It was during those road trips that I first met Florence, Tony's first wife. She was a small, pretty woman with prematurely gray hair that made her look much older than she actually was. She loved to read and I never saw her without a book in her hand.

She was very shy and preferred to let Tony have the spotlight. He was great at it and she enjoyed watching him. I knew them both for over thirty years of their fifty-four year marriage, and I never saw a moment where they weren't devoted to each other. It was one of the strongest marriages I've ever seen.

During the last ten years of that marriage, however, Florence became ill with cancer and Tony was forced to divide his time between the two things he loved most: Florence and his work. He eventually found a balance by

Tony's first wife, Florence, mid-1940s. Their marriage was the strongest I've ever seen.

refusing to accept any job that would keep him out of New York City for more than two weeks.

I remember many times seeing Tony hurry home at the end of the day to cook for the two of them. He often told me dinner was their favorite time together. They'd open a bottle of imported French wine, listen to *Tosca* or some other classic, and share the simple, private pleasures of their life together.

During her illness, Florence always had a nurse with her. This was not only to help her with the day-to-day

Tony and Florence circa 1942.

concerns, but also to build up her strength so that every four weeks she and Tony could go out to dinner and the theatre. Tony used tell me how Florence would barely make it back home before collapsing. Still, I knew it was worth it for both of them.

Watching him with Florence in her last years confirmed everything I wanted to believe about this man—that he was more than just *obligated* to the people and things in his life, but deeply *devoted* to them. Whether it was his work, his family, his theatre company, or his friends, Tony greeted them with full passion and full commitment. I think it was his greatest gift: giving everyone around him permission to love life as much as he did.

I know Florence depended on Tony to lift her spirits and I believe, more than any medicine the doctors gave her, it was Tony's exuberance that kept her alive for so many years. I never talked to her about it, but I think she believed it too.

* * *

Collaborating on *The Odd Couple* with Tony forced me to work at the top of my craft. For example, I was always good at improvising, but I never enjoyed it very much; that is, until I improvised with Tony. He was the kind of an actor who would do a lot of the work for you if you knew how to follow him.

You see, what most actors call improvisations really ends up being a lot of empty talking to fill in the awkward gaps. What Tony taught me was that really good improvisation is about *provoking* the other actor into a response.

For instance, one time I had to teach Tony football and in the script it simply said: "Jack teaches Tony football" at the top of a page and four blank pages followed. Now, Tony knew the game of football even though Felix did not (in fact, what most people would never guess about Tony was that he was an avid sports fan). So, when I got into the three-point football position and said to him, "Let's squat down," Tony knew that he should be facing me.

However, he chose to squat *alongside* me, which provoked me to say, "We're not the Rockettes." Then, after I put him on the opposite side, facing me, he lightly touched his face against mine, which provoked me to say, "I don't want to dance with you, Felix."

If Tony had just stood there, intellectually trying to understand the game of football while I explained it to him, neither of us would've gotten a laugh. But because Tony threw his whole body into the bit and kept prodding me, I was forced to respond, and it set the whole scene in motion.

Sometimes, we would improvise like that for hours while the writers would take notes on what we did. The next day they would come back with something more refined. Then we'd improvise on top of what they had written and the process went on like that until the day of the performance.

Another important principle that Tony and I worked with during *The Odd Couple* was properly motivating the characters. The monk episode (one of my favorites) is a great example of what I mean.

The writers of this episode had started in the middle of the story: they wanted to get Oscar and Felix to a monastery because they knew that once we were there, it would be funny. The problem, of course, was how to get these two hard-bitten New Yorkers to such an unlikely location. Or, in acting terms, how were Tony and I going to motivate this story line in way that was believable for our characters?

We started with the goal of making a larger point about disillusionment with the daily grind and the search for inner peace.

Okay. That was a good theme, but it was still not a motivation. We had to figure out what would drive us to a monastery; what would be the catalyst?

So, finally, we came up the answer. We set it up that Felix and Oscar were having a miserable week. The early part of the show followed them through a couple of fiascos, particularly Felix, who had a kid break one of his expensive cameras and an old lady punch him for trying to help her cross the street. By the end of the week, Felix and Oscar arrived home exhausted and on the brink of a shared existential crisis.

Now we were ready for the doorbell to ring. I opened it and there was a monk in the doorway looking for a contribution. When he saw how tired Felix and I were, he offered to make us dinner in exchange for a ten dollar donation. While he was making dinner, he told us that he was a former executive of an ad agency and one day, while living the daily grind, he looked out of his window and saw a bluebird. He realized at that moment that he

The Odd Couple, *1972 "The Odd Monks."*
By far, one of my favorite episodes!

was a prisoner in his own office. That's when he quit and went to find inner peace at a monastery. Felix suddenly exploded:

"I remember you!" he said. "I worked for you!"

Felix identified with the stress that this former ad executive had been under and concluded that the monastery was the place for him, too! You see, we didn't arbitrarily bring the characters to a monastery. We *motivated* them. This is true of every episode we worked on. Once Tony and I were certain the motivation was honest and consistent with our characters, we left the rest to Garry and the writers who always, always made it funny.

After we'd rehearsed for about three days, I would inevitably say to the writers, "This is funny guys, but where is the love scene?" The first time I said it, they looked at me like I was crazy. The network was already a little concerned about "two grown men sharing an apartment" and so for me to say "where's the love scene?" was almost over the river of good taste. Of course, I didn't mean it literally.

What I was saying was that every show had to have one scene where I told Felix that I loved him but couldn't live with him; or a scene in which he told me, "Oscar, I love you but this time you've gone too far." The reason for this goes back to the first lesson I learned when I watched Walter talk about Felix as "my oldest and dearest friend."

As I said before, I knew in that moment that these two people had to love each other if the show was going

The Odd Couple, *1974 "Last Tango in Newark." Tony dragged me into this improvisation. Afterwards, I said "no more tights!"*

to hang together. I felt this was particularly true of the series, as most sitcoms end up looking the same—silly plots, empty jokes, and unmotivated characters.

The mandatory "love scene" made us real to each other and gave the show a life beyond the situations and jokes. I keep hitting on this point because I'm hoping this book will be read not only by fans of the show, or by fans of Tony and me, but also by young actors and writers who must understand that the most basic unit of any success-ful dramatic truth is human feeling. Not a quick joke, not a clever premise, not a multi-million dollar explosion can outperform a single human emotion. So much of the work Tony and I did together, so much of the success we had, was based on that premise.

The show got cancelled every season and so we were all pretty happy when we reached the 100th episode. We would shoot fourteen more before we were cancelled for the last time.

7 Faces of Dr. Lao, 1964. *Tony played seven different characters seamlessly in this little known gem.*

CHAPTER 5

The Many Faces of Tony Randall

J oe E. Lewis used to tell a story about his piano player: "He'd been with me for twenty years and I didn't know he drank until he came in sober one day." The analogy is relevant to Tony not because he was a drunk, but because there were so many sides to him that I continually found myself surprised by a different aspect.

For instance, Tony loved fine wine, but he also loved a glass of ice-cold beer. He could enjoy French food at Le Cirque 2000 that I couldn't even pronounce, but he could also lick his fingers with the best of them after a box of Kentucky Fried Chicken.

If you went to an art museum with Tony, he could

teach you more in two hours than you could learn at the Louvre in four days. Then on the ride home in the cab he'd tell you the best and dirtiest joke you'd ever heard, all the while laughing that bawdy, infectious laugh.

His relationship to money was the same way—anything but consistent. Don't get me wrong, Tony was never cheap and he was always the first guy to pick up a check, but he could be very tight with a buck for a small thing at noon, and then spend money at night like a playboy. If there was an opera in Milan he wanted to see, he'd tell his wife to pack up and they'd go on a lark. However, paying retail for fine wine was unacceptable. Instead, Tony bought "futures" in French wineries to keep his cost to a couple of bucks per bottle. I'm sure that the day he died his closets were brimming with cases of inexpensive, world-class French wine!

Another example: Tony was usually in good spirits and very supportive of the people around him, but he also had a nasty temper. Now I'm no one to talk because I've always been a hothead myself, but it surprised me to see it in Tony. He always seemed so refined and well-spoken that I imagined he didn't need to yell. But I saw him let it loose on a couple of occasions in a way that surprised everyone.

Elinor Donahue related a story about this at the memorial tribute in October 2004. She explained how she was always nervous on the first camera day and that often made her slow to react. Tony didn't say anything about it all day, and then suddenly exploded at her:

"Pick up the cues! Pick 'em up! What are you—a professional or an amateur!"

I remember the situation vividly and I could tell that Elinor was not only scared and surprised, but also mad. As she told it, she remembered thinking "Well, I'll probably never work on this show again. And I don't know if I want to."

The next day she arrived at her dressing room only to find it filled with flowers and apologies.

I remember another time there was a big guy on the set taking pictures of us. We had never seen him before, but we were on a protected lot, so we assumed that he had the authority to be there. However, he never officially came up and introduced himself or explained his purpose.

Anyway, he kept coming in very close while Tony and I rehearsed. We were having some trouble with the scene just as this poor bastard came too close for the last time. Tony suddenly broke off from the scene we were working on, walked over to the guy, turned him around, and practically threw him out the stage door.

Like I said, this was very big guy—about six-four and real stocky. I couldn't believe it as I watched Tony reach up—way up—to grab this giant by the scruff of the neck and escort him out.

The next day, Tony went to a lot of trouble to find out where the guy lived. He called him personally to apologize for losing his temper.

I don't know why, but he never lost his temper with me. Even if he had, it wouldn't have bothered me. I'd seen him get angry enough times to know that just as the last angry word left his lips, he would instantly feel remorse.

That was Tony: complex, passionate, contradictory. But in the end always kind.

Complex. Passionate. Contradictory.

The Odd Couple, 1971, "Hospital Mates." When I found this
picture, I was struck by the image of Tony smiling at me from
across a hospital room. He was such a big part of my comeback
from cancer that this image seemed to tell the whole story.

CHAPTER 6

Overcoming Cancer

In 1989, I was rehearsing in Los Angeles for a revival of *Twelve Angry Men*. I was thrilled to be working on it again because this time I was playing the role my idol, Lee J. Cobb, originated when we did the movie together forty years earlier.

During rehearsals, however, I noticed that at certain pitches my voice generated no sound. This frightened me because many years before I had undergone radiation treatment for throat cancer.

The first time I got cancer was when I was performing in *The Odd Couple* on stage and I was constantly getting laryngitis. I put off going to the doctor for a long time but when I finally did, he told me that I had leukoplakia, a dangerous pre-cancerous condition.

"If you stop smoking now," the doctor told me "it will probably disappear. If you don't, in a year I'll be taking out your vocal chords and that will be the end of your acting career."

I stopped smoking that minute and after three months, I went back for a follow-up visit. This time the doctor told me that I had "virginal" vocal cords again— not a mark on them. So, what did I do? I left his office, went down the pharmacy that was in the building, and bought a pack of cigarettes!

Anyway, fast-forward ten years to the rehearsals for *Twelve Angry Men*. We only had one week left of rehearsal, so I hurried to see my doctor about the crack in my voice. After the examination, he told me he saw something on my larynx that bothered him. He decided to perform a biopsy.

Two days later, he called me and told me that I had invasive throat cancer and said that I must undergo surgery immediately. I didn't like that word: *invasive*. What did that mean? I felt fine! I had no discomfort, no laryngitis, and I felt no pain whatsoever! I asked him if the operation could wait for about six weeks because I really wanted to perform this role in *Twelve Angry Men*.

"Jack," the doc told me plainly, "It's invasive." There was that word again. "That means it's very aggressive. If we don't cut it out right away, in three months you'll be short of breath and in four you'll be dead."

Nothing echoes like a diagnosis. It has the sound of a bell that has been rung so hard, it cracks.

So, I left the show and flew to New York to have the operation at Mount Sinai Hospital. My doctor, Dr. Max Som, who had been my main ENT (ear, nose, throat) man for years, said he was too old to operate, but that he'd found this "kid" with "golden hands."

Max explained to me that me he would still be present in the operating room, but this kid would perform the actual operation. The goal was to cut the cancer out, but leave my larynx intact. My voice, everybody understood, was my livelihood.

Dr. Hugh Biller was that kid, and he did have golden hands. He performed a sensational operation. The problem was that once they were inside, it became apparent my condition had worsened to the point where they had to cut a little deeper than planned. The result was that my right vocal cord was reduced to a stump and the cause of preserving my full voice had been lost.

After the operation, I was crushed by the news. Sure, I had beaten the cancer, but I had no voice at all, no sound! I could only whisper. I felt like John Henry, the horse, who had earned six million dollars while racing. The day he had to stop, he was not only worthless—he

An old drawing of me, circa 1960. Note the cigarette.
It never left my hand for forty years. Don't Smoke!!

was a liability. He was a gelding who couldn't reproduce. I was an actor who couldn't speak.

The first friend to visit me in the hospital was Tony Randall.

"You're going to be fine," he reassured me.

I gestured to indicate how angry I was about losing my voice! He smiled and moved a little closer.

"Hey, let's face it, Jack," he kidded me gently. "You never did sound like Richard Burton."

I couldn't actually laugh, but I smiled enough to let him know I appreciated the humor. Then he got very serious, looked me right in the eye, and said, "Jack, if you ever feel like going back to work, I will find a venue for us. And you know I mean it."

I did know he meant it and I appreciated the thought, but I felt lost! Overnight, I had gone from being at the height of my powers, rehearsing for one of my favorite plays, to this: a gelding in a world of studs. Acting had been my best friend for so many years and now, suddenly, traumatically, my best friend had been taken away.

For a while, I was angry and bitter. I remember watching television soon after the hospital stay and saw that a New York Mets pitcher had lost his right arm to cancer. His right arm! The one thing he needed most! I got so mad. "It's not fair!" I gurgled at the television set. "I don't need my right arm and you don't need your voice! Why can't we trade?"

Of course, that's not how things work in this world.

But I didn't care. I continued to rage for about three weeks until I suddenly realized that I wasn't playing the hand that I'd been dealt. Sure, I could sit around and blame God or the Fates, but it still wasn't going to give me my voice back. So, I stopped. I still sulked a lot, but I stopped shrieking in whispers.

Six months later, the American Cancer Society called me to be a spokesperson for a function they were having in Atlanta, Georgia. They wanted me to present the *Tree of Life* to hundreds of cancer survivors and their spouses. They also wanted me to make a speech.

"Are you nuts?" I asked.

"We know you have no voice and have difficulty speaking," they replied.

"Difficulty speaking?" I gasped. "Gimme a break!"

"Actually, it's your celebrity status that we're interested in," they confessed. "Your presence would mean a great deal to those survivors." I wondered why. Why would my speech make any difference to them? Who the hell was I to them, or them to me for that matter?

Up to that point in my life, I hadn't let anybody see me vulnerable, not even my children. Why should I start now? In fact, I'd always made it a point, throughout my entire life, to never ask anybody for anything. As far back as age six, I shined shoes for spending money so I wouldn't be obligated to anyone. I sold pretzels for a penny a piece for lunch money. When I wanted a bicycle, I sold subscriptions to *Colliers*, the *Saturday Evening Post*, and the *Ladies Home Journal*. All through my life, it was this way. It was how I protected myself. As a result, I was a gracious *giver*, but a lousy *receiver* of love.

Well, in spite of myself, I let them talk me into going. I agreed to be the guest of honor at the Cancer Society event as long as they didn't want to *give* me anything. If my celebrity status could offer people a little inspiration, great. It sure as hell wasn't doing me any good.

So, I flew to Atlanta, Georgia, but with trepidation in my heart. I couldn't shake an uneasy feeling about the American Cancer Society event. As soon as I landed in Atlanta, I knew why: it was over one hundred degrees with ninety percent humidity. I knew the event was to take place outside and when I actually got there, my worst fears were confirmed: there was no shade anywhere and it was topping out at *one hundred and three degrees*. Man, this event was off to a bad start—and so was my attitude.

What I didn't know was that the heat was going to be the least of my problems because just as I approached the podium to speak, the PA system broke down!

I couldn't believe it! No microphone, no voice, just me standing in front of a large, expectant crowd of people with no way to communicate. I was talking but no one could hear me. It was like a bad dream. What made it worse was that with all of the ambient noise, I couldn't even hear myself.

I was so mad. I hated myself for agreeing to come. I

hated the American Cancer Society for asking me to come. I hated the survivors and their spouses; and now, to top it all off, I had to present the *Tree of Life* to these people!

There must have been five hundred people there and every one of them wanted to meet me. They came toward me two at a time; the survivor and their spouse, and I was supposed to congratulate them and give them a *Tree of Life* placard.

When I saw the people lining up, it took all of my strength not to run. The only thing that kept me there was my word. I had made a promise to stay for the entire evening and I couldn't, *wouldn't* ever break it.

Then, something completely unexpected started to happen. It was a small thing, but it would change my life. I realized that after I had given out about five placards that I was starting to feel better. In fact, as more and more people came toward me the good feeling I had increased. I suddenly started listening to what people were saying as I gave them the *Tree of Life*: "We love you, Jack," they said, or "You look wonderful, Jack," or "We prayed for you," or "You're gonna make it through this, Jack."

Maybe it was because I was needy, I didn't know; but these people I had hated a minute ago were suddenly helping me. What was it? What had happened so suddenly that I felt hope again and connection?

Before I had even finished asking the question, I got the answer. Not one of the people who approached me that day, not one in five hundred, had used the pronoun "I." Not one came up to me with self-pity or complained about the way *they* felt or looked for *me* to save *them*. On the contrary, every single one of those people, *except* me, was thinking about someone else! In that instant, I knew what it meant to be a cancer survivor.

I was so overcome with feeling that I had to excuse myself. I ran to the nearest men's room where I had the second happiest cry of my life. Then I left my pity pot right there in that bathroom—where it belonged—and went back out to the event.

They took two hundred and fifty pictures of me that day and my smile was genuine in every one of them.

I decided to become a spokesperson for the American Cancer Society, and I traveled all over the world—to Guam, to Europe, to Asia—telling total strangers my story and listening to theirs. It was a great experience as we all became brothers and sisters in a battle for our lives.

National Actors Theatre production of Neil Simon's
The Sunshine Boys, *1998.*

CHAPTER 7

Tony's National Actors Theatre

"Every civilized nation in the world has a classical repertory theatre which is the pride of its nation. France has La Comédie Française; Israel, the Habima; Japan, the Kabuki; Ireland, the Abbey Theatre in Dublin; Russia, the Moscow Art Theatre, and the list goes on. And yet, the United States has none. This is not only a crime, it is a scandal."

—Tony Randall, 1991

The National Actors Theatre was Tony Randall's baby and he loved it with all of his heart. It was a huge dream and for years I listened to him talk about it:

Tony and me with Abe Vigoda rehearsing
The Odd Couple *Benefit Performance for the N.A.T., 1991.*

an *American* theatre company, dedicated to the classics, that would deliver world-class theatre in a way that was accessible and affordable to everyone. It would have a large educational component, integrating theatre into school curriculums and it would treat college students like welcomed guests. The funding was going to come from corporate donors who would see the light of Tony's vision and therefore would give generously and frequently.

Personally, I never thought it would work. It was so

pie-in-the-sky that I just wrote it off as someone chasing windmills. That's the way Tony thought: Big. Passionate. Impossible. He really was a Don Quixote that way.

But even I made the mistake of underestimating him because Tony would spend the next decade bagging nearly every windmill he chased. Until in 1991, I saw him fully realize his dream of a National Actors Theatre. It was quite a sight. This skinny little kid from Tulsa, Oklahoma, had manifested an entire institution!

He acquired the seed money by giving up his salary from various acting jobs, asking that people simply make an equivalent donation to the National Actors Theatre. It was a brilliant plan that worked beautifully and it allowed him to put together a sensational staff, now headed by Fred Walker. Fred was Tony's right-hand man and is still there doing all of the brilliant, tireless work of keeping Tony's dream alive.

From top to bottom, it was exactly what he wanted it to be and he was part of everything that happened there—from designing the season, to acting, to directing, to working with the students. Tony poured his soul into the National Actors Theatre and it got real results. To date, the National Actors Theatre has produced twenty-one plays and exposed over 40,000 New York high school students to the very best theatre in the country at absolutely no cost to them.

I once built a horse ranch in the desert and it damned near killed me. What Tony had done was miraculous.

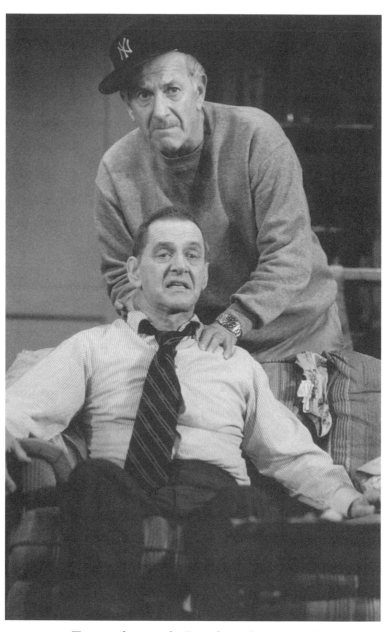

Tony and me in the Benefit Performance of
The Odd Couple *for the N.A.T., 1991.*

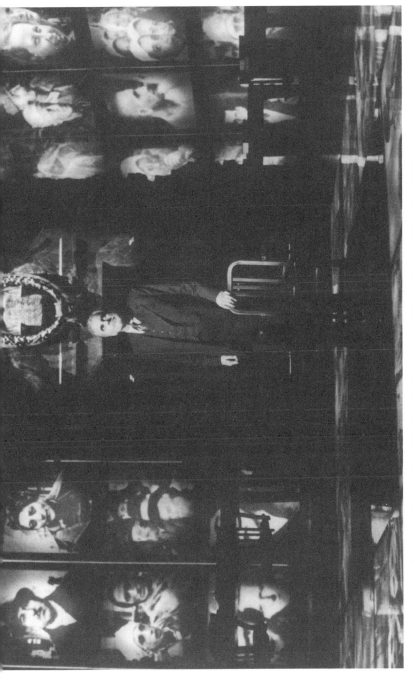

Maximillian Schell in Judgement at Nuremberg, N.A.T., 2001.

Matthew Broderick and Judy Parfitt, Night Must Fall,
National Actors Theatre, 2001.

*Julie Harris and Charles Durning, The Gin Game,
National Actors Theatre, 1997.*

That's why neither of us understood why he got such a lukewarm response from the New York press. They were supportive of the *idea*, but stingy with Tony, as if they were reluctant to take him seriously. It really caught him off guard. He fully expected that the press in a major theatre town like New York, a town so starved for substance, would *flock* around a National Actors Theatre dedicating itself to the classics.

I'm not saying Tony wanted a free pass from the critics just because he was doing a good thing. Tony could choke down a bad review with the best of them but often the New York critics would go out of their way to make it personal. They tried to belittle what he was doing, as if it were a junior effort—a *"television"* effort.

It was a cheap shot. They had simply made up their minds about Tony before he ever opened the theatre: he was an upstart, a television entrepreneur on an ego trip. Of course, nothing could have been further from the truth. But it still hurt Tony, although he rarely showed it.

No matter what anybody says, I know the truth: Tony Randall was a giant in the New York theatre scene. His effort was super-human and whether the critics wanted to acknowledge it or not, the National Actors Theatre is the best thing to happen to that town since the public library. Aside from his children, it is his proudest legacy.

So, to settle the score, I'm including in this book a list of plays the National Actors Theatre has performed over the years. I have also included a list of the prominent actors who appeared in the productions. It becomes clear right away that Tony, and not the critics, won the war for a legitimate National Actors Theatre.

NATIONAL ACTORS THEATRE CHRONOLOGY

1991-1992 Season

The Crucible by Arthur Miller
Starring Martin Sheen, Fritz Weaver, and
Michael York

A Little Hotel on the Side by Georges Feydeau
Starring Lynn Redgrave, Tony Randall, and
Rob Lowe

The Master Builder by Henrik Ibsen
Starring Lynn Redgrave and Earle Hyman

1992-1993 Season

The Seagull by Anton Chekhov
Starring Tyne Daly, Jon Voight, Laura Linney, and
Ethan Hawke

Saint Joan by George Bernard Shaw
Starring Maryann Plunkett, Jay O. Sanders, and
Michael Stuhlbarg

Three Men on a Horse by George Abbott and
John Cecil Holm
Starring Jack Klugman, Tony Randall, and
Jerry Stiller

1993-1994 Season

Timon of Athens by William Shakespeare
Starring Brian Bedford
(Tony nomination for best revival of a play)

The Government Inspector by Nikolai Gogol
Starring Tony Randall and Lainie Kazan

The Flowering Peach by Clifford Odets
Starring Eli Wallach and Anne Jackson

1994-1995 Season

Gentlemen Prefer Blondes, book by Anita Loos and
Joseph Fields, adapted from the novel by Anita Loos

1995-1996 Season

The School For Scandal by Richard Brinsley Sheridan
Starring Simon Jones

Inherit the Wind by Jerome Lawrence and
Robert E. Lee
Starring George C. Scott and Charles Durning
(Tony nomination for best revival of a play)

1997-1998 Season

The Gin Game by D. L. Coburn
Starring Julie Harris and Charles Durning
(Tony nomination for best revival of a play)

Othello by William Shakespeare
(Co-production with Royal National Theatre
and Brooklyn Academy of Music)

1998-1999 Season

The Sunshine Boys by Neil Simon
Starring Jack Klugman and Tony Randall

1999-2000 Season

Night Must Fall by Emlyn Williams
Starring Matthew Broderick and Judy Parfitt

2001 Season

Judgement at Nuremberg by Abby Mann
Starring Maximillian Schell and George Grizzard

2002-2003 Season

The Resistable Rise of Arturo Ui by Bertolt Brecht
Starring Al Pacino, Tony Randall, John Goodman,
Steve Buscemi, Chazz Palminteri,
Billy Crudup, Dominic Chianese, and
Paul Giamatti

The Persians by Aeschylus, adaptation by
Ellen McLaughlin
Starring Len Cariou and Roberta Maxwell

2003-2004 Season

Right You Are by Luigi Pirandello, translation by
Eric Bentley
Starring Tony Randall

New York, opening night of the National Actors Theatre.
This skinny kid from Tulsa had manifested an institution!

Opening night, The Odd Couple,
National Actors Theatre Benefit Debut, 1991.
It was the first time I'd been on a stage since my cancer diagnosis.
People had coughed up over a million dollars for this performance.
I felt doomed to disappoint them.
Left to right: Jack Weston, Martin Sheen, me,
Tony, and Abe Vigoda.

CHAPTER 8

How Tony Gave My Life Back

Three years after the operation, I heard the tabloids were going to publish a story saying that I was dying. It was not true. I wasn't going to work anymore, but I had beaten the cancer.

I didn't want my friends to worry about me, so I called *Entertainment Tonight*. I offered them an exclusive if they would send Jeannie Wolf to interview me. She was a pal of mine and I knew I could trust her. We did the interview and I let my friends and fans know I wasn't dying.

Gary Catona, a voice builder, saw me on *Entertainment Tonight* and contacted me. Gary had been a trained opera singer and had worked with a terrible teacher who ruined his voice. It was then that he turned to the study of voice reproduction and worked with a doctor to develop his own approach to voice rehabilitation.

"I think I can help you," Gary told me over the phone.

I wanted believe him, but it was hard. There was barely a sound—a whisper—at this point in my recovery.

"Are you a doctor?" I whispered.

"No," he replied.

"Then how are you going to help me?"

"Come to my office and we'll talk."

I took Gary up on his offer and spent an entire hour in his office as he tested my voice in various ways.

At the end of the session, Gary said, "I think I hear a sound."

"I think you hear money," I told him.

He laughed.

"What have you got to lose?" he said.

I thought about it. He was right. I had nothing to lose at this point but a few bucks. So, for the next four months straight I did these strange, almost violent voice exercises under Gary's direction. A part of the process was intense vocalization, and the other part was educating me on what needed to happen.

Normal vocal cords have two sides that come to-gether in the center and touch. The touching of the two chords produces the sound of a normal human voice. In my case, the center of my right cord had been removed and was now a stationary stump. Gary explained to me that vocal cords are muscles, and that if we could make my left cord strong enough, it might stretch beyond the center and touch what was left of the right cord. If that happened, my voice would produce a sound. It seemed like science fiction to me, but as Gary said, "What did I have to lose?"

Over time, these violent, unorthodox vocal exercises had some success and I started to hear a tiny sound. Almost on cue, I received a phone call from Tony.

"Jack, Tony calling! Listen. If we could do a one-night theatre performance of *The Odd Couple* on Broadway we could raise a million dollars for the National Actors Theatre."

"Tony, what have you been smoking?" I asked. "Can you hear my voice? I can barely talk to you on the phone, and you want me to get on a stage?"

"Precisely!" Tony said.

"Don't hold your breath." I told him and hung up.

Laughingly, I told Gary about my conversation with Tony. Gary immediately said, "Tell him you'll be able to do it in six months."

"Gary, c'mon," I said. "I've made some good progress here, but let's not kid each other. I'm not ready now, and I won't be ready in six months."

"Tell him you'll do it, Jack!" he said, ignoring me. "I promise you'll be ready."

I was shocked by how serious Gary was about it. Was

it possible? Could I be ready in six months? That was the question I carried around for the next couple of days. I kept going back and forth. On the one hand, boy did I want to do *The Odd Couple* with Tony, particularly on behalf of the National Actors Theatre!

On the other, I needed to be realistic. I've always taken pride in being a pragmatist and I demand brutal honesty from myself and others—it wasn't going to happen. The pragmatist had spoken and it was final.

That is, until the gambler took over.

One morning I woke up and before I realized what I was doing, I found myself dialing Tony's number. As soon as he answered the phone, I placed my bet: "Tony, it's Jack. My voice coach says I'll be ready in six months."

"That's perfect!" Tony replied. "It'll take me that long to get publicity going and everything set up. Welcome back, partner!"

So, for six months I worked on my voice like Rocky worked on his body. Every day I took steam, exercised my vocal cords; even when I drove the car I did my exercises. Slowly, the whisper became a sound, and in time, the sound became a little voice. But was it enough to perform on Broadway?

During rehearsals, the other members of the cast treated me as though my voice was normal. I didn't realize then that they were only being nice, because I wanted to believe them. I was fooling no one but myself.

Then suddenly, it was opening night. I didn't feel

ready and I found myself in the presence an old but familiar dread. The audience had coughed up one million, two hundred-and-fifty thousand dollars for this performance. Some people paid twenty-five thousand dollars for ten seats and a table at the dinner afterward. I felt doomed to disappoint them.

Waiting backstage to go on, my heart was beating so hard I thought it would break through my skin, just as it had at Carnegie Tech when I performed *One Sunday Afternoon*. In my mind, I could draw a straight line between that moment and this; only this time I knew I was going to fail. You don't get that lucky twice in one lifetime.

The play started, and before I made my entrance there were eight minutes where four guys with normal voices were playing poker. I was offstage listening to them get big laughs and I could barely breathe.

Suddenly, it was the time for my entrance. I went on stage, said my first line, and I heard the audience shifting uncomfortably in their seats. I instantly panicked. The calmness I had found at Carnegie Tech was gone and just like at the Cancer Society, I couldn't hear myself; only this time it was because my heart was pounding like a pile driver. My legs felt like they might buckle. And even though I was wearing a microphone, I was sure the audience couldn't hear me, either.

"My God," I thought. "What the hell was I thinking when I decided to do this play? How am I going to get through the next *two hours?*"

From the moment I stepped onto that stage, I was in a free fall. I had to finish the play, but I didn't know how I was going to do it. But then I heard Murray the cop ask me what I had to eat. I turned toward him and like a veteran prizefighter on the ropes, all I could do was keep my legs under me and throw a reflex punch.

"I've got brown sandwiches and green sandwiches," I said.

"What's the green?" Murray asked me.

"It's either very new cheese or very old meat."

The audience laughed. They actually laughed. So, now I knew they could hear me. Then I got another big laugh, and then one more. And then I heard the audience take a deep breath and relax back into their seats. I did the rest of the play and got all the laughs I had gotten when I did it originally. What a tremendous relief!

Now, I have not mentioned what Tony Randall was doing during the performance because I wanted to save the best for last. Only *I* could see that Tony had one goal that night; he had chosen one action to play, and that was to support me.

In the play, Felix would yell at me for being sloppy and inconsiderate, but Tony's eyes would light up every time I got a laugh. They'd say, "Go, Baby! Go! I knew you could do it." And for those two hours, he was my anchor, my Rock of Gibraltar. I will always love him for that.

At the end of the play, we received a two minute standing ovation. I grabbed Tony and thanked him as the

*Celebrating with my family after the benefit. From left to right:
My younger son Adam, his wife Nancy, my older son David,
Brett Somers (yes, my ex!), and Tony on the very end.*

curtain went down. Then the stage manager ran over to
us and said:

"Don't you hear that?"

"Hear what?" I asked.

He brought the curtain up and not a soul had moved.
The audience was still standing, still applauding. They
wanted another curtain call. We started crying. They
started crying. And for seven minutes on Broadway, there
was a genuine lovefest.

In the audience were two women with whom I had worked—Sylvia Sidney and Helen Hayes. Together, they represented about 160 years in the theatre.

Sylvia turned to Helen and asked, "Have you ever been to a theatre where you've seen such love transfer itself from the audience to the stage and back?"

"I have never seen such love in the theatre, period." Ms. Hayes replied.

When I walked into the post-theatre party, Tony introduced me as "the gutsiest son of a bitch in the world."

"I'm not the gutsiest son of a bitch in the world," I said. "I'm the luckiest son of a bitch in the world to have a friend like Tony Randall."

Tony took no credit. And he would not accept my thanks.

"No, you did it," he told me.

"No!" I kept insisting. "I would never have had the nerve to get back on the stage if it hadn't been for you! You gave me my life back!"

It has remained the most glorious night of my life.

* * *

After that gala benefit show of *The Odd Couple*, Tony's enthusiasm kept me going to do more plays. Yet despite that glorious night, I was still scared. My voice was, and is, not a normal voice. Tony was undaunted. "I'm going to find another play for us," he told me.

Soon afterward Tony called me and said, "How about *Three Men on a Horse?*"

"I thought you only did classics," I told him.

"This is an American classic," he said, "and we're gonna do it!"

Scared or not about my voice, I jumped at his offer. In fact, I could hardly wait for another chance to get back on the stage, and another chance to work with Tony. He had also gotten commitments from what would prove to be a wonderful cast, including Julie Hagerty, Joey Faye, and Jerry Stiller. I really was the luckiest son of a bitch in the world.

I was particularly excited about working with Jerry again because I had admired him long before he was George Costanza's father on *Seinfeld*. When we were young men, I'd done two plays with him and in one of them Jerry took on a very serious, dramatic role and absolutely blew me away. From that play forward, I always thought of him as a young Paul Muni. Who knew he was such a great comedian?

Anyway, when it came time for rehearsals, I noticed that something had changed for me. I was not the loner I had been so many years before. I allowed myself to get involved with the people around me. I even invited Jerry Stiller to lunch!

However, I stopped doing my vocal exercises during rehearsals because I thought I was saving my voice by not doing them. It turned out the opposite was true and my voice was getting weaker. The director was concerned, but he was afraid to say anything. Even Tony, who was

The cast of Three Men on a Horse, *1993,*
National Actors Theatre.

always honest, wasn't sure how to approach me. Finally,
he just came out and told me. I had suspected it, but hear-
ing it from Tony shot a lightning bolt of fear through me.
I went back to doing my vocal exercises the same day.

Then a strange thing happened. After a few weeks,
my voice came back, but something was different. It
seemed stronger than it had been before—much stronger.
I should have been reassured, but it was *so much* better
that I couldn't ignore the fact that something had
changed. You'd think I would just stay quiet and not ask

too many questions, but I actually felt a little afraid. I needed to know what was going on down there!

So, I went back to the doctor. He looked down my throat and smiled.

"First off, the cancer is gone. Completely. So, don't worry about that. And second, you got a lucky break."

Apparently, a piece of cartilage had broken loose and fell into a perfect position inside my larynx. Now I had even more control and a lot more power when the cord hit it. It wasn't a perfect voice, it definitely wasn't my old voice, but it was a voice. And it was enough to keep me acting.

When I left the doctor's office that day, it was like I'd graduated somehow, like my second chance had been made official.

Tony was so pleased with my new projection he kept trying to talk me out of using the microphone. I would have none of it. That mike was like my magic feather, and I needed to know it was there. Tony gave in for a while, and ultimately it was Richard Fitzgerald, a terrific soundman and very dear friend, who made my voice sound acceptable on stage.

But Tony couldn't let it go. One day he finally said, "Look, after the show today I'm going to ask the audience to stay. We'll do a scene from *The Odd Couple* without mikes and see what happens."

"Okay, Tony," I told him. "But if it flops, then never again!"

We tried his idea. The audience stayed and Tony and I did the scene where Oscar is complaining to Felix about the infuriating notes that he writes.

"You leave me little notes on my pillow." Oscar says. "'We are all out of toilet paper—F.U. It took me three hours to figure out that F.U. was Felix Unger."

The audience roared.

Later, Tony pressed his point. "See, you don't need it!" I knew he was right, but I still used that microphone. Sure, it was a crutch. But in my mind, it did what all crutches do—it kept me from falling on my ass!

The only real negative experience I had with the National Actors Theatre was on opening night for *Three Men on a Horse*. A second-rate critic for the *New York Times* showed up and wrote in his column that I should get out of the business because of my voice. It hurt me a little at first, but I knew the truth, so I really didn't care what he said. Tony, however, was livid.

"It's a cheap shot!" he screamed.

"So, what's new? He gets paid by the cheap shot," I said. "And anyway, he's the one who should get out of the business because he obviously doesn't know a hit when he sees one!"

And it turned out I was right. Tony and I had the last laugh. *Three Men on a Horse* was a big box office hit and the National Actors Theatre's first profit maker.

* * *

One day, the phone rang: "Jack, it's Tony." The voice was

somber. I immediately knew something was wrong.

"What's the matter?" I asked.

"Could you be in New York on Thursday? The Actors Theatre is having a board meeting—" He paused for a minute. "I need you there."

Apparently, the theatre desperately needed more money and I could tell Tony was feeling discouraged. He had already thrown nearly eight million dollars of his own money at the National Actors Theatre and still it wanted more. It was becoming clear that its appetite for cash was bottomless.

Then I had an idea. For a long time, I'd wanted to find a way to repay Tony for standing by me so faithfully and here was my chance. I made him an offer he couldn't refuse.

"Why don't we take *The Odd Couple* on the road for eight to ten weeks without drawing a salary, and give the money to the theatre?" I said.

Tony was silent for a minute.

"You would do that, Jack?" he said, surprised. Like I wasn't indebted to him, like he wasn't the guy who had saved my life.

"Of course! It'll be like the old days! We'll have a blast!"

"You're a gem, you know that?" Tony said. "A gem!"

After I hung up the phone, it occurred to me that it wasn't just professional between us anymore—it was *personal*. We were there for each other in a way that we'd

Old buddies.

never been before and it seemed to grow directly out of the night of my comeback. I realized that I'd never trusted another person as much as I did Tony that night. Trusting someone changed me somehow. I wasn't exactly sure what had happened to me. I only knew I felt different.

We took the play on the road to cities like Cleveland and Boston and packed them in. We had a great time together, took no salary, and donated every penny to the National Actors Theatre. In all, we generated nearly one million dollars for the theatre and I felt like I had made some headway toward paying Tony back.

Tony never stopped looking for plays for us to do, but it had to be the right fit. We even experimented with Samuel Beckett's *Waiting for Godot* but it didn't feel right. We tried out some of the English plays that Sir Ralph Richardson and Sir John Gielgud had done; but they didn't work for us either.

Then, in 1997, the phone rang. "Jack! Tony calling!"

Like I didn't know.

"I've got it!" he cried. "How about *The Sunshine Boys?*"

I knew the play. It was another great one by Neil Simon and I said yes immediately.

The play centers on two old vaudevillians who have to stop arguing with each other long enough to do a skit for a television special. Tony thought he was right for the part of Willie Clark. I didn't picture him in that role and I told him so. I thought he should play the part of Al Lewis. Neil Simon agreed with me and that cinched it. I played Willie Clark. Tony was Al Lewis.

The funny part about doing the play was that we were older than the characters. But when it came time to rehearse, Tony and I would dodder around stage like old men. Finally, John Tillinger, the director, stepped in and stopped us.

"What are you doing?" he asked us.

"What?" I said.

"What's with all the doddering?"

"These guys are seventy years old," Tony said.

"Well, how old are you, Jack?"

"About seventy-five," I told him.

We still weren't getting it.

"Gentleman," he said, "both of you are *older* than these characters, but neither of you are stumbling around!"

Tony and I looked at each other and laughed. We didn't think of ourselves as old, even without our toupees, but we were. It was a real shocker. From then on we played these guys as old, but not arthritic.

One of my favorite things to watch during *The Sunshine Boys* was the tea stirring scene. It's a great example of what I admired about Tony's acting technique. He could take a simple thing, like stirring a cup of tea, and get the absolute maximum amount of juice from it.

In the script, it says that Al Lewis is stirring a cup of tea *ad nauseam*. Now I would've done it for a few beats and moved on quickly because it's a dangerous bit. If you don't commit to it and really play the silence, no one will know what's going on and the joke will be lost. If you milk it too much, it sucks the life out of the next six minutes of the play and you may never catch up.

Seeing Tony was like watching a master jazz musician. And that's exactly how he played it—like music. He knew just how many times to stir the tea, how many times to clink the spoon against the cup, and he knew just where the silences were that would drive me nuts.

"Enough, already," I used to think when we were on

The Sunshine Boys, *National Actors Theatre*, 1998.

stage. "You're gonna kill the joke." But the audience loved him and laughed along with every minute. Sometimes he would take so long that I couldn't tell if it was Jack Klugman or Al Lewis who was frustrated.

Then, just when I thought it was finally over, he would add some sugar to his tea and start stirring it all over again. The audience would laugh themselves out of their seats. It was an instinct Tony had, this precise little voice inside his head that told him how far he could go to get the most out of every scene. I watched him do it for thirty-five years and I never stopped being amazed.

ARTHUR F. & ALICE E. ADAMS THEATRE
COCONUT GROVE PLAYHOUSE, MIAMI, FLORIDA

Rough Crossing *program, 2002.*

The last play Tony and I did together was Tom Stoppard's adaptation of Ferenc Molnar's *The Play's the Thing* known as *Rough Crossing.*

I hated it.

We did it in Florida, and the average age of the audience was about ninety-five. They didn't really understand the play, they really didn't understand my asides, and one person actually yelled at me from the audience. Every night I expected some old lady to break out the tomatoes and start throwing them at us. Tony didn't care. He loved the play. It was English and he got to wear a cravat and sing.

I didn't know it then, but that would be the end of the road for us.

CHAPTER 9

Heather and Tony

I first knew Heather Harlan as an intern at Tony's National Actors Theatre. Later I knew her as a fellow actor in *Three Men on a Horse*, the play that Tony and I starred in for his theatre company.

Heather was a pretty, ambitious young girl with a lot of talent. But, to tell the truth I was more concerned about my lack of a voice than I was about Heather. Evidently, Tony was not. I had no idea that they had a relationship blossoming, even though my dear girlfriend Peggy Crosby tried to tell me that they were a twosome. So, a little while ago, Burton Rocks interviewed Heather. Here's the way she remembered Tony.

Burton: When did you first meet Tony?

Heather: *I was an intern at the National Actors Theatre. I had great respect for Tony because I admired his acting. I tried to be cute with him, but he kept shooting me down. One night, I called my father and told him what a jerk Tony was, and that I was thinking of quitting. But the next day Tony apologized to me and was so nice that I felt guilty about calling my father.*

Burton: Why were you attracted to Tony, after all he was fifty years older than you?

Heather: *How do I make anyone understand? He was like a God to me. He could talk about music. He could talk about art. But then he could also talk about baseball statistics. He knew who pitched in the 1957 World Series. He was the smartest person I had ever met, but he was also funny. Believe it or not, it is very difficult to find a guy who is both bright and funny. Tony was both. The difference in our ages may have bothered him, but I never gave it a thought. He was a rare man, and I was lucky to have had him as long as I did.*

Burton: What was Tony's credo? What was most important to him?

Heather: (Thoughtfully) *Gosh, there are so many things. But I guess they're all tied to honor—honoring*

A very happy family. From left to right:
Julia, Tony, Heather, and Jefferson.

others, *honoring your heart, standing strong with*
your family, respecting others.

Burton: What did he consider his greatest achievement?

Heather: (Laughing) Oh, *that's easy—our children. He felt*
they were his greatest achievement. He was proud

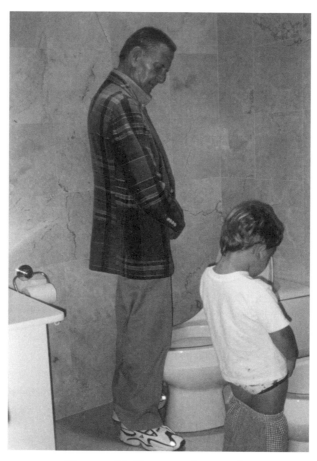

*Tony and Jefferson make time for
a little male bonding.*

*of his theatre, but when it came to the children—
oh, they overshadowed everything.*

Burton: What were the parts of Tony that made up the
whole, total, man?

Heather: (Again laughing). *That would take me forever.*

*Julia loved the opera and she and Tony
would sing arias together . . . in Italian!*

*Like all interesting men, he was complicated; he
was full of contradictions.*

We would usually dine at the best and most expensive restaurants in New York and he never gave the cost a thought. And yet, if he got a fan letter where the post office didn't cancel the stamp, he

*would carefully remove it and use it on one of the
letters he would send.*

*One trait I really admired was the way he
bounced back from adversity. He had tremendous
strength of character. No matter how many times
he got knocked down, he always got right back up.*

Burton: Was Tony a hands-on father? Did he interact
with the kids?

Heather: *Maybe not like today's generation, but he was an
excellent father. He was home a lot and he would sit
in this big chair and read; and the kids took comfort
knowing that when they came home from school he
would be there. He introduced Julia to the opera,
and he'd sit on the floor in Jefferson's room and he'd
build LEGO towers with him.*

*You know, I never saw him lose his temper, or
his patience with them. He was always loving and
warm. He adored them. He felt they were a gift he
never expected to get. They miss him terribly, even
though they're so young. Whenever I think of all
the knowledge he would have imparted to them, all
the culture, it makes me very sad.*

Burton: Did he ever talk about Jack Klugman?

Heather: *Oh, incessantly. He always talked about him. He
admired him. He thought Jack showed a lot of forti-
tude when he did that benefit performance of* The
Odd Couple *after he had lost his vocal cord.*

I think they brought out the best in each other. They were competitive with each other, but in a positive way. If you didn't see them in The Sunshine Boys, *you missed a real treat.*

Burton: How long after you started dating Tony did you get married?

Heather: *About two years, I guess. We lived together for a year.*

Burton: How did Tony propose to you?

Heather:(Laughing) *It was very unromantic. I wanted to get married but he kept worrying about what people would say about our age difference, and then he got sick with the flu; I took care of him. I always took care of him, but I guess his being laid up and everything made him see things more clearly. He said, very casually, "All right, let's get married." We were going to go to city hall, but a friend said, "You two can't just go to city hall and get married. I'll get Mayor Giuliani to marry you." Mayor Giuliani was a good friend of ours, and he spoke beautifully at Tony's funeral. Anyway, he married us.*

Burton: What was it like to be married to Tony?

Heather: *It was comfortable, very comfortable.*

Burton: Were children in your plans?

Heather: *Not before we got married, but once we tied the knot and discussed it, we decided to try. We never*

*thought we'd be successful. But I thank God we
were.*

Burton: How did he react when you told him you were
pregnant?

Heather: *Typically—the reality that he was going to be a
father both surprised and delighted him. We were in
London where he and Jack were doing* The Odd
Couple *at the Haymarket Theatre. Jack loves
telling this story. The night I told Tony I was pregnant Jack said Tony knocked on his dressing room
door and when Jack opened it, Tony stood there
grinning from ear to ear and said, "The machinery
works!"*

Burton: Did Tony ever talk about the fact that he would
not live to see them grow up?

Heather: *Sometimes he would talk about it, but not in a
melancholy way. See, he didn't know how much he
would love them. He discovered that, and so he
wanted to share with them the different stages of
their lives. He didn't want them to forget him; that
was very important to him. I'll see to it that they
don't.*

Burton: What activities did they do together?

Heather: *He took Julia to the opera and to Tony's surprise she
loved it. He would take her backstage to meet the
singers. In fact, she would ask him to take her to the*

opera. He taught her some arias and they would sing duets in Italian at the dinner table. It was impressive. Jefferson, on the other hand, loved toys and games. Tony would get on the floor and play with him for hours at a time.

Burton: He sounds like a hands-on father to me.

Heather: Yes. *Now that I talk about it, I guess he was a hands-on father. He even took them to the Yankees baseball games, hot dogs and all.*

Burton: Did the children know how sick he was? Did they visit him in the hospital?

Heather: Yes. *They visited him quite often. At first, they were scared. He was very thin and they had never seen him so weak. But, after a few visits, they got used to how he looked and were just happy to see him. Tony never took his eyes off them; he even smiled when he could.*

Burton: Did they realize that he might not recover, that he might die; or were they too young?

Heather: *They were too young. When the doctor told me how ill Tony really was, I gently told the kids because I wanted to prepare them for whatever might happen. Well, my God. They didn't know what life was. How could I expect them to understand death? When Tony died, Jefferson said he was going to get a special machine that would take him to Heaven to see his father. Julia just refused to deal with it. She was in denial, but now we talk about it. Julia is beginning to accept his absence. Jefferson is still very angry.*

Burton: How about you? Have you coped with his death?

Heather: *I've just lived. I get up in the morning and just live my life. When you go through something like this, you really find out who your friends are. Many, many people were there for me and I love and appreciate them all. Some people were not so nice and, honestly, I appreciate them too because they forced me to be stronger. They forced me to grow up. I miss him. I miss everything about him: his wisdom, his strength, his humor, but mostly his love.*

The proud father.

The Sunshine Boys, *closing night, 1998.*

CHAPTER 10

"Jack, Tony Calling!"

B efore Tony went into the hospital, Peggy and I flew to New York and saw him rehearse the Pirandello play *Right You Are* for the National Actors Theatre. He sat on the side with his eyes closed, as though he was sleeping. When he heard his cue coming, he jumped up with a burst of energy that lasted only as long as the scene. When the scene was over, he sat back down and closed his eyes again. The other actors were excellent, but when Tony stepped into the scene, I could feel the hair rise on the back of my neck.

He had a *presence*. Now, you can't *acquire* presence. You can't *fake* it, and you can't *learn* it from any acting teacher. You've either got it or you don't. And Tony had it in *spades*.

The Pirandello play received good reviews, especially Tony. Thank God the critics stopped attacking him personally and just assessed his performances. It was a six-week run and Tony hung in there, even though he wasn't feeling well. After the fifth week, though, he started to experience severe chest pains.

During a checkup, it was discovered that he had heart trouble and they decided to keep him in the hospital. They ended up performing heart surgery but then his kidneys stopped functioning so he was placed on dialysis. The problems were mounting.

Even with all these health problems, everyone still expected him to recover. There was something inexhaustible about Tony and I too expected him to pop up again, like he had done at the Pirandello rehearsal. But it wasn't going to happen this time.

I arrived at the hospital and met Heather in the hallway. She braced me for what I was about to see.

"Be prepared," she warned. "This is not the Tony you knew."

I walked into the room and what I saw was shocking.

From left to right: Me, *Peggy Crosby, Heather Randall, and Tony, at an event before Tony became ill.*

Tony was very, very thin. He had almost no strength, and for the first time he looked really, really old. He smiled when he saw me, and that made me feel great. I did most of the talking, of course, and he answered me with nods. Then, out of the blue, he said, almost rudely, "You don't have to stay, you know. Why don't you go!"

I couldn't believe that even now he felt he was imposing on me. But like me, Tony was a great giver, but a lousy receiver of love.

"So, you're trying to get rid of me already, huh?" I said, roughly. "I'm not going anywhere. I flew three thousand miles to see you and I'm staying right here!"

I could tell he was pleased. He had just been trying to let me off the hook. Still, it was truly amazing that after all he had done for me when I needed him, it was still hard for him to accept me being there for him in his time of need.

Anyway, Heather and I knew that Tony was going to be in the hospital for quite a while, so when the American Cancer Society was giving him an award, Heather asked me to substitute for him. Of course, I said yes.

She also asked me to sit in as the host of the Gala, which was an annual event to raise money for the National Actors Theatre. I had attended many of them, but only as a guest. This time I had some big shoes to fill, so I wrote to all of the participants explaining that I, and not Tony, would be hosting the Gala this year.

Two weeks later Peggy and I were back in New York for the event. I asked Garry Marshall to accept an award. As always, his speech was hilarious. For a while, we all managed to feel as if our dear friend was there with us.

Later, when Peggy and I visited him in the hospital (which we did quite often) the reality of what was happening to Tony was painfully clear. He thanked me for replacing him that night. I told him that replacing him was impossible. I was merely substituting for him. He liked that.

The Gala turned out to be very successful and we raised about eight hundred thousand dollars. Tony liked that, too. For a while afterward, Tony rallied a little bit: some color came back his cheeks, and he started talking about getting out of the hospital and going home. We were all encouraged.

Then, on one visit, I met Heather outside his hospital room. She asked me to try to get Tony to consent to an operation. It seemed that the water that they usually drained from his lungs had become solid and they needed to do some surgery.

I talked to him about it, but he seemed resolute.

"Hey, you've got to get well so we can do another play together," I persuaded him. "I haven't been in a hit since we did *The Sunshine Boys*."

But this time Tony didn't smile. It was not a good sign.

Heather rubbed his forehead and she pleaded with him to consent to the operation. Then the doctor talked to him as well. Finally, the three of us surrounded his bed and barraged him with the reasons to sign the consent, and finally he did give his consent.

I kissed his forehead, said goodbye, and went back to Los Angeles with Peggy.

I didn't know it then, but that was the last time I would ever see Tony alive.

The operation did not go well. In fact, once the doctors opened him up they saw that his organs had ceased to function and they knew then the situation was hopeless.

Hopeless—a word I had never heard Tony utter. Hopeless was just not in his vocabulary. It was a sad word on which to end such a rich and happy life.

And Tony's was a happy life. I mean let's face it, how many of us get a chance to live our lives in two acts? In act one, Tony was a rising star with a shining career and a fifty-four year marriage that was loving and devoted. In act two, he married a talented young actress who adored him, became a philanthropist, and had two gorgeous children he loved more than anything. I mean, how many of us can say we lived so well?

Still, there was a deep sadness I couldn't shake.

The first memorial was at a funeral home. There were lots of people, both celebrities and non-celebrities, all talking about Tony in the past tense. I was still confused. Like I said at the beginning, I couldn't accept that Tony was really gone. I knew that my phone would ring when I got home and Tony would be on the other end, energetically saying, "Jack! Tony calling!" I knew that as sure as I knew that I was an actor. So, why did the rabbi speak so eloquently about Tony, as though he were gone? Heather, too? And Eli Wallach and Cliff Robertson and Mayor Rudy Giuliani? What were they talking about?

I found myself disbelieving them all until Sherrill Milnes, the opera star from the Met and Tony's dear friend, got up to sing a hymn. He sang it with his soul. That's when I lost it; tears erupted from me in an explosion of grief, and I finally accepted that my dearest friend had, in fact, died.

Then, it was my turn to speak. I pulled myself together and went to the podium, determined not to cry. I spoke of a woman who had seen me earlier and said that she saw something in me that reminded her of Tony. I replied that it would be impossible; like finding a moment of refinement in a Brian De Palma movie. Tony's friends laughed. I said that if I did have any class, Tony put it there.

Then I finished by telling them about my favorite episode of *The Odd Couple*: "Password." It was also one of Tony's best ad libs. In the episode, Tony lost a game on *Password*, but refused to leave the set. Finally, the security guards had to carry him out, and as he was being dragged away, Tony improvised, "Boy! What a gyp!"

Well, that's how I felt the day Tony died—gypped. But why? What was this feeling that kept following me around after his death? Like I said, Tony had enjoyed a double scoop of life, cherries and all, and I been there for the best parts. So why did our relationship not feel complete?

I pondered over it for weeks, trying to understand my grief. When I finally came up with the answer, it explained a lot, not the least of which is why I felt so compelled to write this book. You see, I hadn't ever told Tony the real gift his friendship had given me. It had very little to do with *The Odd Couple* or the National Actors Theatre or throat cancer, those were just the circumstances we lived under. The real gift that Tony's friendship gave me was the capacity to truly trust another human being completely. And that single act changed my life.

Up until I was diagnosed with cancer, I had spent seventy-five years living like a hermit inside myself. It didn't matter who I was with, even my family, I had a strict policy that people simply could not be trusted. And I don't mean trusted with money or things, those are easy to lose because they can be replaced. I'm talking about trusting someone with feelings. Growing up in such a tough neighborhood with repressed Jewish immigrants taught me to protect myself at all costs. The problem was that no one ever told me exactly what it was I was protecting.

Honestly, I would never have trusted Tony that much if I hadn't needed him. But I did. I wanted my acting career back after throat cancer more than I had wanted it the first time. If I was going to get it, I would be forced to trust him. That meant another human being would see me vulnerable and scared and weak as I struggled to stand on my acting legs again. I would have to let myself need Tony's support. I would have to rely on him to help build me up again. And most importantly, I would *owe* him something. The problem was I'd spent my entire life—*my entire life*—making sure that I never, ever owed anybody anything.

Life's funny, isn't it? Because when I consider all that

The second memorial.
Making my final wish for Tony.

I gained because I was forced to let Tony help me, I can't help but wonder about what I missed during all those years I lived in a shell. And that's the feeling I couldn't shake after Tony died— the sense that I'd lost more than a dear friend. For over a month, I had the distinct feeling that I'd also lost years that would never come back.

And so, I'm grateful to Tony not just for being the best acting partner I ever had, or for being the first in line on the other side of my operation, or for starting the National Actors Theatre, or for even for helping me win my career back—he knew I appreciated all of those things. What I didn't get the chance to tell him was that our friendship had made me a better human being. It made me a better father. I let my children inside now and I'm not afraid to let them see me as I am. Throat cancer was the wake up call—accepting Tony's friendship and generosity was the beginning of an honest answer.

I don't like to preach, but I'm going to now because I

feel this is too important not to say. If you're like I was, or you're someone who likes to hold a grudge, or you've never really let someone know what they mean to you because you're afraid, ask yourself this question: what are you really protecting? If you look, you'll see it: nothing. Absolutely nothing. Just phantoms from old wounds that never healed. Give them up and join the people in your life who love you. Risk it all. For me, it was the best gamble I ever made.

***

The second memorial for Tony Randall was less formal. It was held at the Majestic Theatre on Forty-fourth Street between Broadway and Eighth Avenue. It was for the public. Sixteen hundred seats were filled with friends and fans. Hundreds were turned away. Tony would have been pleased with the turnout. He also would have been pleased with the talented people that spoke so glowingly of him. People like Julie Harris, Paul Newman, Harry Belafonte, Mayor David Dinkins; all had been deeply impacted by Tony and showed up that day to bear witness to his passing.

I was the final speaker. I told some funny anecdotes about Tony and then got a little serious with everybody. I said I had been given three wishes in this life, two of which had already been granted. The first wish was that I would become an actor. The second wish was when I lost my voice, I would be given a sound so that I could go back to the theatre I loved.

"And now," I announced, "I am going to make my third wish: someday soon I will be walking down Broadway and look up to see a sign in lights that reads: THE TONY RANDALL THEATRE. Underneath it will be a placard that reads: PERMANENT HOME OF THE NATIONAL ACTORS THEATRE.

Then I will know *for absolutely certain*—Tony Randall rests in peace.

Tony Randall 1920–2004

An Interview with
Jack Klugman

Q: What inspired you to write *Tony and Me?*

A: When Tony died, I just couldn't accept it. The sadness stayed with me for weeks. I've had to watch plenty of friends die over the years—that's one of the downsides to getting older. But with Tony I felt differently and it took me some time to understand why. In a lot of ways, *Tony and Me* has been a process of figuring it all out.

Q: What conclusions did you reach?

A: That friendship is something people undervalue. I know I did. For years, I took the people in my life for granted. But when I got throat cancer, it turned out that they were all I had. All of a sudden I could count the people I trusted on one hand. Tony was on that very short list. And not just for that first flush of catastrophe, but from beginning to end—first friend through the hospital door and the last one to leave.

Q: In the book you talk about this. You even have a chapter entitled "How Tony Gave My Life Back." What do you mean?

A: My other best friend has always been acting. It was my ticket out poverty and it took me farther than I ever imagined it could. When I lost my voice to throat cancer, I lost more than my career, I lost the entire thread of my life. So when Tony offered me the opportunity to perform on Broadway again, at a time when I had almost no voice at all, he took a big risk on me. That experience changed my life.

Q: You made the choice to self-publish. Why?

A: Because I needed to be sure it was done right. I'd never worked with a large publishing house, but I instinctively didn't like the idea of handing *Tony and Me* over to someone I didn't know. My friendship with Tony is a very personal thing.

Q: Is that the only reason?

A: That . . . and the money! [Jack laughs to himself]. I wanted to keep more of it, sure, but mainly so I could give some of it to The National Actors Theatre. It's as important a cause now as it was when Tony first started it. I very much want to help keep his dream alive.

Q: There's a DVD that comes with the book, right?

A: Yes. And it's hysterical. Paramount Studios has been very generous to let us include a reel of outtakes from *The Odd Couple*. Even though I lived it, the footage still makes me laugh every time I see it. I think it's going to be a real treat for fans of the show.

Q: If you were going to describe the story of *Tony and Me* to a friend, what would you say?

A: I would say that Tony and Me is the story of a successful professional relationship that became very personal. But it's also my story. And Tony's story. But mostly, I see *Tony and Me* as a simple story about friendship itself—a small tale of two men who took fifty years to figure why they came together.

Jack Klugman was interviewed at his home in Malibu, California, May 24, 2005.